SCHOLASTIC

NAVIGATING NONFICTION

by Alice Boynton and Wiley Blevins

Credits appear on pages 111–112 which constitute an extension of this copyright page.

Copyright © 2007 by Scholastic Inc. All rights reserved. Published by Scholastic Inc. Printed in the U.S.A.

ISBN-13 978-0-439-78298-2
ISBN-10 0-439-78298-8

SCHOLASTIC and associated logos and designs are trademarks and/or registered trademarks of Scholastic Inc.

1 2 3 4 5 6 7 8 9 10   40   15 14 13 12 11 10 09 08 07

Table of Contents

UNIT 1

Reading Nonfiction
LESSON 1
Look What Animal Teeth Can Do! 4
Alaskan Animals Change
With the Seasons! 5

LESSON 2
A Wampanoag Homesite 7
Oh Wow! A Powwow! 8

Text Structure: Problem/Solution
LESSON 3
Endangered Animals Get Help 10

UNIT 2

Text Feature: Special Type
LESSON 4
Animals Need Trees 14
What's in a Rain Forest Tree? 15

LESSON 5
Stamp of Excellence 17
Honoring Our Past Heroes 18

Text Structure: Compare/Contrast
LESSON 6
Meat-Eating Plants! 20

UNIT 3

Text Feature: Diagrams
LESSON 7
Space Suits 24
Pilgrim Children 25

LESSON 8
Hard Workers 27
Groundhog Burrow 28

Text Structure: Description
LESSON 9
Columbus's Trip 30

UNIT 4

Text Feature: Flow Charts
LESSON 10
From Grapevine to Jelly Jar 34
Making Crayons 35

LESSON 11
It's a Frog's Life 37
How Ladybugs Change and Grow . . . 38

Text Structure: Sequence
LESSON 12
Take a Trip, Butterflies! 40

UNIT 5

Text Feature: Captions and Labels
LESSON 13
Just Add Water 44
Seeds on the Go! 45

LESSON 14
Flag Day 47
Chinese New Year 48

Text Structure: Cause/Effect
LESSON 15
Amazing Rain 50

UNIT 6

Text Feature: Headings
LESSON 16
Women Inventors 54
Women Scientists of Today 55

LESSON 17
Those Amazing Spiders 57
How Animals' Body Parts
Help Them Survive 58

Text Structure: Problem/Solution
LESSON 18
Today's Cool Fire Tools 60

UNIT 7

Text Feature: Maps
LESSON 19
Weather Watch 64
Weather in Our Country 65

LESSON 20
Helicopters Help Out! 67
My Dad Is a Park Ranger 68

Text Structure: Description
LESSON 21
Be a Dino Detective 70

UNIT 8

Text Feature: Charts
LESSON 22
Chocolate Comes From Trees 74
What Comes From Trees? 75

LESSON 23
Water in Winter 77
The Power of Weather 78

Text Structure: Compare/Contrast
LESSON 24
Before They Were Presidents 80

UNIT 9

Text Feature: Graphs
LESSON 25
Let's Vote! 84
Meet Gary Soto 85

LESSON 26
Hot Days, Cool Animals 87
Zoos Help Out 88

Text Structure: Cause/Effect
LESSON 27
Kids Help the Earth 90

UNIT 10

Text Feature: Time Lines
LESSON 28
Martin Luther King, Jr. 94
My Story by Ruby Bridges 95

LESSON 29
Great Inventions 97
Great Scientists 98

Text Structure: Sequence
LESSON 30
Guide Dog Lessons 100

ADDITIONAL MATERIALS

Let's Navigate 104
Text Structures 105

Graphic Organizers
Sequence 106
Compare/Contrast 107
Cause/Effect 108
Problem/Solution 109
Description 110

Reading Nonfiction

Nonfiction gives you facts in many different ways. There's the main article, of course. But there may also be facts in photos, captions, labels, and maps. Sometimes there's so much stuff on the page, you might not know how to begin. Here's how!

Step 1 Preview the article to get set for what you will read.
The article below is about animal teeth. You learn this by reading the title.

Step 2 Read the article.
This article is about the teeth of a walrus.

Step 3 Read the added information.
This article has a photo of walrus tusks. The label tells us that they are tusks, or walrus teeth.

Practice Your Skills!

1. Underline the title.

2. Circle the boldfaced word.

3. Put an **X** on the label.

PAIR SHARE How does a walrus use its teeth?

Look What Animal Teeth Can Do!

Different animal teeth have different functions.

When a walrus wants to get out of the water, it uses its teeth to help! The walrus pushes its long teeth, or **tusks**, into the ice. Then, it pulls itself out of the water and onto the ice.

tusks

Practice Your Skills!

Before You Read

Preview the article. Check (✔) the special features it has.

__ title
__ photos
__ boldfaced word
__ graph
__ map

As You Read

• Did you read the title?
❏ Yes ❏ No

• Did you look carefully at each photo?
❏ Yes ❏ No

• What did you learn from each photo? from the map?

After You Read

1. How did the headings help you remember the facts in the article?

2. What did the photos compare?

PAIR SHARE Why is the map included? How does the color help?

Alaskan Animals Change With the Seasons!

Autumn

Winter

In autumn, the arctic fox's brown fur helps it hide in brown grass. It can sneak up on prey. In winter, the fox's fur changes to match the snow. That way, it can still sneak up on prey.

Autumn   Winter

In autumn, the grizzly bear eats and eats. It puts on fat for winter. In winter, the bear **hibernates**, or sleeps deeply. It doesn't eat. Instead, the bear lives off its fat.

On Your Own

Look at this page about sound. You can make it easier to read. Here's how:

Step 1 Write a title.

Step 2 Read the article.

Step 3 Draw a picture of each animal. Label part of the animal.

Title: _____

Many animals use sounds to communicate with each other, just as people do.

Mice

Mice make very high sounds. They are too high for people to hear. But a mother mouse can hear her lost baby's sounds. The sounds help her find her baby.

Humpback Whales

Humpback whales hear high sounds, too. Their sounds are like songs. The songs reach whales that are 500 miles away! Whales use echoes to find their way around underwater.

Reading Nonfiction

Nonfiction gives you facts in many different ways. Sometimes there's so much stuff on the page, you may not know where to begin. Here's what to do!

Step 1 Preview the article to get set for what you will read.
This article tells about the Wampanoag.

Step 2 Read the article.
This article is about an outdoor museum. It shows visitors how the Wampanoag Indians lived long ago.

Step 3 Read the added information.
This article has a photo of a canoe.
The caption tells how the canoe was made.

Practice Your Skills!

1. Underline the title.

2. Circle the boldfaced word.

3. A canoe is a kind of _____.

PAIR SHARE If a map had been used, what might it show?

>>€€ >>€€ >>€€ >>€€ >>€€ >>€€ >>€€ >>€€ >>€€

A Wampanoag Homesite

The Wampanoag (wam-puh-NO-og) have lived in Massachusetts since before the Pilgrims came. Today, some Wampanoag teach people how they lived long ago. They teach people at an outdoor museum.

Mishoon (mih-SHOON) This is the Wampanoag word for **canoe** (kuh-NOO). They made canoes by burning out logs. They used canoes for travel and fishing. Some canoes could hold up to 40 people!

>>€€ >>€€ >>€€ >>€€ >>€€ >>€€ >>€€ >>€€ >>€€

Practice Your Skills!

Before You Read

Preview the article. Check (✔) the special features it has.

__ title
__ boldfaced word
__ pronunciation
__ chart
__ photos
__ map

As You Read

• Did you read the title?
  ❏ Yes ❏ No

• Did you find Kansas on the map?
  ❏ Yes ❏ No

• How did you read this article?

After You Read

1. What is another word for **powwow**?

2. Why was the grass dancer first?

PAIR SHARE Which powwow dance would you like to do?

OH WOW! A POWWOW!

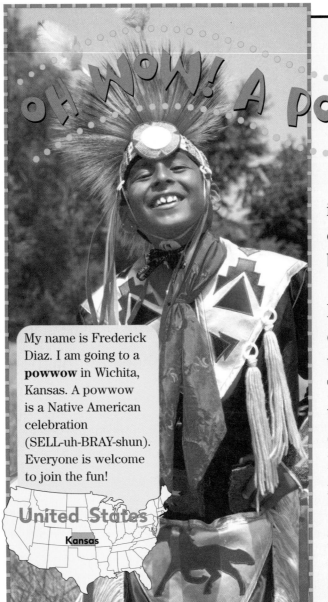

My name is Frederick Diaz. I am going to a **powwow** in Wichita, Kansas. A powwow is a Native American celebration (SELL-uh-BRAY-shun). Everyone is welcome to join the fun!

United States
Kansas

This is me! I dance in the powwow dance contest. I move to the beat of the drums.

I am a grass dancer. In the old days, grass dancers were the first to dance at powwows. They would stomp the tall grass down so that others could dance. Now, people use lawn mowers!

I sometimes win money for my dancing. Today, I came in second place!

Three More Kinds of Powwow Dancers

fancy dancer

hoop dancer

jingle dancer

On Your Own

Finish this article. Here's how:

Step 1 Write a title.

Step 2 Use labels or captions.

Step 3 Make new or hard words **dark** to look boldfaced.

_____
(title)

In 2005, the world's biggest plane was made in Europe. It is called the A380.

The jumbo jet holds 800 people. Its tail is seven stories tall. The A380 has a roomy lounge, or sitting room. And some of these huge planes will even have beds! Welcome aboard!

LESSON 3

Problem/Solution

Text Structure

Practice Your Skills!

Before You Read

Vocabulary Use these and other words to fill in the web.

endangered   oryx

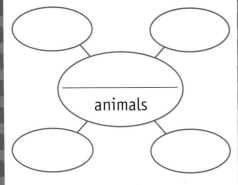

animals

As You Read

Text Structure Read to find out each **problem**. As you read, circle the **solution**.

Text Features The writer helps you understand the information. Notice that pronunciations help with new words and labels name animals.

After You Read

1. Why do some animals become endangered?

2. Which solution do you think was the smartest? Why?

3. How could some of the solutions help other animals?

Endangered

Many animals are endangered, or close to dying out forever. See how endangered animals, like the Florida panther, are getting the help they need.

Florida Panther

Problem People built roads through the panther's home. When the panthers cross the roads, they get hurt by cars.

Solution People built tunnels under the roads where the panthers cross. Now the panthers can pass safely—*under* the roads.

Animals Get Help

Kemp's Ridley Sea Turtle

Problem People throw big nets into the ocean to catch shrimp. Turtles get caught in the nets and can't get away.

Solution Now all nets must have a special opening that lets turtles swim away.

Arabian Oryx

Problem People hunted the oryx (OR-iks) until there were almost none left.

Solution Zoos came to the rescue. They took the oryx that were left and kept them safe. In the zoos, many baby oryx were born. Soon there were enough oryx to safely let them go back into the wild.

Grizzly Bear

Problem People cut down most of the forests where grizzly bears used to live. The grizzly bears need the forests for food and shelter.

Solution Now there are protected national parks where the grizzly bears can live. In these forests, the grizzly bears find plenty of food and shelter.

Problem/Solution

Reread "Endangered Animals Get Help." Fill in the graphic organizer.

Problem	Solution
Florida panthers were getting hurt by _____.	
Sea turtles were getting caught in _____.	
Trees where grizzly bears live were _____.	
Most of the oryx were gone because people _____ them.	

Writing Frame

Use the information in your organizer to fill in the writing frame.

Many animals are endangered, or in danger of dying out.

The Florida panther is in danger because _____

_____. To solve this,

_____.

The sea turtle is in danger because _____.

To solve this, _____

_____.

The grizzly bear is in danger because _____

_____. To solve this, _____

_____.

The oryx is in danger because _____. To solve this,

_____.

 Use the writing frame as a model to describe three problems with owning and caring for a pet. Tell how each problem could be solved.

Special Type

Take a look at your science book. You will see all kinds of **special type**. There are **boldfaced** words, words in *italics,* and words in (   ). There are words in different SiZes and different colors. Why?

Words in special type stand out. They say, "Look at us!" That's because they are clues to help you understand what you read. So use the clues!

Step 1 **You can't miss the title. It's BIG! It tells what the article is about.**
The article explains why animals need trees.

Step 2 **Pay attention to the boldfaced words.**
They are important words about the topic. Be sure you know what they mean.

Step 3 **Use the pronunciation tips.**
The writer tells you how to say a word that may be hard. The writer puts a pronunciation tip in (   ) after the word.

Practice Your Skills!

1. Underline the title.

2. Circle the **boldfaced** words.

3. Put an **X** on the pronunciation tip.

PAIR SHARE Look at each picture. What animals use trees in that way?

Animals Need Trees

Some animals live on a tree in a nest.

Some animals live inside a tree in a **den**.

Some animals use a tree to build their home, such as this beaver's **lodge** (loj).

Some animals eat the seeds of trees.

Some animals drink the **sap** of trees.

Some animals eat the fruit of trees.

Before You Read

Preview the article. Check (✔) the special features it has.

__ title
__ photos
__ labels
__ boldfaced words
__ pronunciations
__ map

As You Read

- How many **boldfaced** words do you see?
  ❏ 2   ❏ 3

- Did you study the photos and labels?
  ❏ Yes   ❏ No

- Why does **kapok** have a pronunciation tip?

After You Read

1. How did the pronunciation tips help you?

2. What does **prey** mean?

PAIR SHARE What plants live in the rain forest? How are they different from plants where you live?

WHAT'S IN A RAIN FOREST TREE?

The **kapok** (KAY-pok) tree is one of the tallest kinds of rain forest trees. You can find them in Costa Rica. So many plants and animals can be found on just one kapok tree. They use the kapok for different reasons.

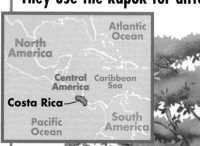

harpy eagle and young

The harpy eagle makes its nest at the top of the tall tree. From all the way up here, it can watch for **prey** (pray) to catch. It brings back a meal for its young to eat.

margay

The margay cat hunts for small animals in the tree. It climbs up and down the tree trunk. It crawls through the branches. The cat's wide eyes search for climbing mice and rats to eat!

orchid (OR-kid) plants

These plants grow on tree branches instead of on the ground! They grow up here to reach sunlight. The forest floor is too dark for them to grow.

two-toed sloth

The slow sloth visits the kapok tree. It eats the leaves. It hangs around the branches. Then, it goes to another tree to eat more leaves.

poison dart frog

The frog climbs up the tree to find a cup-shaped plant. This kind of plant holds a little pool of rainwater. The frog lays her eggs in this little pool.

On Your Own

This page is about birds. You can make it easier to understand. Here's how:

Step 1 Write a title.

Step 2 Use a color to darken important words.

Step 3 Add pronunciations to any hard words. Use a dictionary for help.

_____
(title)

Many of the same kinds of birds act in different ways. Some are shy while others are bold. Why? Scientists are studying the traits of wild birds to find out. Genes, a part of an animal's cells that determine how it looks and acts, cause birds to act a certain way. A bird's traits can help it to survive.

Based on what you read, what is another word for *traits?* What are some of your traits? Make a list of at least five traits.

Text Feature

Special Type

When you look at nonfiction, you see all kinds of **special type**. Some words may be big. Some may be in color. Some may be **boldfaced,** in *italics,* or in parentheses ( ).

Words in special type stand out. Use them to figure out the important words and ideas in the reading. Here's how.

Step 1 **You can't miss the title. It's usually BIG! It tells what the article is about.**

The article below is all about a special stamp.

Step 2 **Pay attention to the boldfaced words.**

These are important words about the topic. If they are new words, be sure you know what they mean.

Step 3 **Use the pronunciation tips.**

A difficult word often has a pronunciation tip after it. The tip in parentheses ( ) tells you how to say the word.

Practice Your Skills!

1. Put an **X** on the boldfaced words.

2. Underline the pronunciation. Sound out the words.

3. What does **issued** mean?

PAIR SHARE Why is this stamp important?

Stamp of Excellence

USA 80
SPECIAL OLYMPICS
2003

The United States Postal Service is showing its Olympic spirit. In 2003, this agency **issued**, or put out, a new stamp to honor the Special Olympics (SPEH-shul oh-LIMP-iks). The **Special Olympics** is a sporting event in which disabled people take part. There are many events, including soccer, basketball, swimming, and gymnastics.

The Special Olympics stamp costs 80 cents. It can be used for packages mailed to places outside the United States.

Before You Read

Preview the article. Check (✔) the special features it has.

__ title
__ boldfaced words
__ pronunciations
__ photos
__ map

As You Read

- Did you read the title to learn the topic?
  ❏ Yes ❏ No

- How many pronunciation tips are there?
  ❏ 1 ❏ 2

- What do you learn from the photos?

After You Read

1. Why is there a statue of Abraham Lincoln?

2. Who was Jackie Robinson?

PAIR SHARE Who have you seen honored on money or with statues? Who would you honor this way?

Honoring Our Past Heroes

Many men and women have made important contributions to the people of the United States. Some ways we **honor** and remember them are by putting their pictures on money or by creating statues (STA-choos).

Susan B. Anthony helped women get the right to vote.

Sacagawea (SAH-kuh-juh-WEE-uh) **guided**, or led, the explorers Lewis and Clark in the West.

Ben Franklin was a scientist and an inventor, and he helped write the Declaration of Independence.

Jackie Robinson was the first African American to play Major League baseball. He also fought for civil rights.

Abraham Lincoln was the 16th president of the United States. He helped end slavery in our country.

On Your Own

Use The Facts to write a paragraph. Add **boldfaced** words and pronunciations. Here's how:

Step 1 Write a title.

Step 2 Make important words about the topic dark to look **boldfaced**.

Step 3 If you think a word is hard to say, add a pronunciation tip. Use the dictionary for help.

The Facts

☛ In 1860, Abe Lincoln ran for president. When he won, he grew a beard. We remember him looking this way.

☛ Lincoln was a great president who helped unite the nation after a long war. This war is called the Civil War. It ended slavery in the United States.

☛ Lincoln kept documents, or important papers, in his tall hat!

☛ Lincoln's face is on the $5 bill.

_____
(title)

_____
_____
_____
_____
_____
_____
_____
_____

 In the box, draw a picture for the article. Label it or add a caption.

LESSON 6

Compare/Contrast

Before You Read

Vocabulary Fill in the chart.

Word	Where Found	Example
nutrients		
tentacles		
ooze		

As You Read

Text Structure The writer of this article **compares and contrasts** a Venus flytrap, a sundew, and a pitcher plant. As you read, underline the words that tell how these plants are different. Circle how they are alike.

Text Features Look carefully at the boldfaced words and pronunciations to help you learn and read new words.

After You Read

1. Why do some plants eat meat?

2. How do the plants get bugs to land on them?

Meat-Eating Plants!

Most plants make food from water, sunlight, and nutrients from soil. Why do some plants need meat? Meat-eating plants live where the soil doesn't have a lot of nutrients. They get their nutrients from insects—like the one trapped inside this Venus flytrap.

tentacle

Stuck on a Sundew!

How It Attracts: At the end of each long tentacle there is a drop with a bit of **nectar**, or sweet liquid, inside it. The sweet-smelling nectar attracts insects.

How It Traps: When the insect steps on the drop, it gets stuck. The drop is sticky! Then the tentacles wrap around the insect, trapping it in more sticky drops.

How It Eats: There are juices inside the drops that turn part of the insect into a liquid. Then the plant **absorbs**, or takes in, the insect's nutrients.

Caught in a Venus Flytrap!

 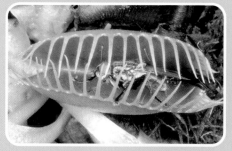 

How It Attracts: The red color and sweet smell of this plant's leaves attract insects.

How It Traps: There are tiny hairs inside the leaves. When an insect brushes against the hairs, the two leaves snap shut.

How It Eats: The leaves ooze a juice that turns part of the insect into a liquid. Now the plant can absorb, or take in, the insect's nutrients.

Fallen in a Pitcher Plant!

How It Attracts: The pool of liquid inside this plant has sugary nectar inside it. The liquid's sweet smell attracts insects.

How It Traps: When the insect lands on the edge of the plant, it slides down the slippery walls. Splash! The insect falls into the pool. It can't get out.

How It Eats: There are juices in the liquid that break down the insect. Now the plant walls can absorb its nutrients.

Fun Facts About Meat-Eating Plants

- Meat-eating plants can trap and eat animals as big as frogs, lizards, and birds.
- Meat-eating plants eat only the parts of the insect that they need. They leave the skeleton (SKEL-ih-tuhn), wings, and antennae (an-TEN-ee) behind.

Compare/Contrast

Reread "Meat-Eating Plants!" Fill in the graphic organizer to show how the Venus flytrap and sundew plant are the same and how they are different.

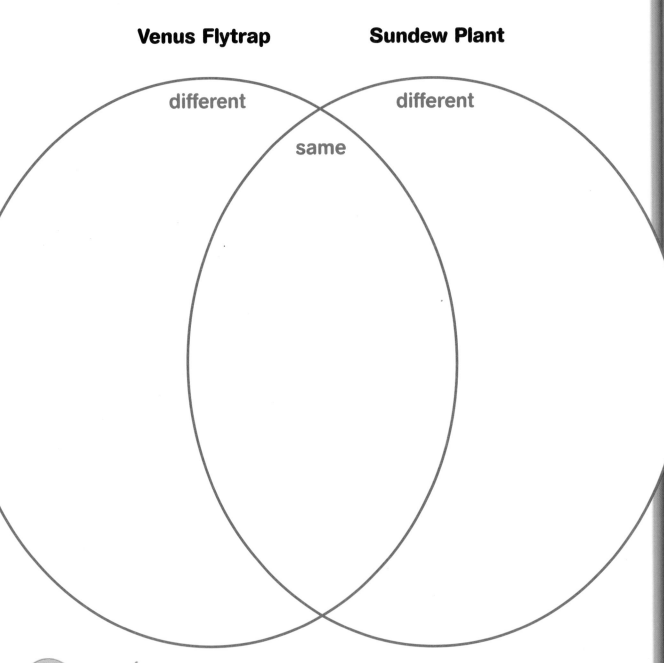

Venus Flytrap   **Sundew Plant**

different   different

same

Use the graphic organizer above to retell "Meat-Eating Plants!" in your own words. Remember to include how the Venus flytrap and the sundew plant are alike and how they are different.

Writing Frame

Use the information in your organizer to fill in the writing frame.

Both the Venus flytrap and the sundew plant are the same in some ways.

They are the same because they both _____.

_____

_____

_____.

However, in other ways the Venus flytrap and the sundew plant are

different. They are different because _____

_____

_____

_____.

So, the Venus flytrap and the sundew plant have both similarities

and differences.

 Use the writing frame above as a model to compare and contrast the sundew plant and pitcher plant.

Diagrams

A **diagram** is a special picture that shows the parts of something or how something works. The diagram helps you "picture" the information and makes it easier to understand. Here's how to read a diagram.

Step 1 **Read the title and introduction.**
They tell you what the diagram is about. The diagram below shows what an astronaut wears in space.

Step 2 **Read the labels. They name parts of the diagram.**
Each label on this diagram tells about a part of the space suit.

Step 3 **Follow the arrows or lines.**
They connect the labels to the picture. Each label is written in or by the part of the diagram it describes.

Practice Your Skills!

1. Circle the title of the diagram.

2. Underline the name of what goes on the astronaut's hands.

3. Put an **X** on the part that protects the astronaut from extreme heat or cold.

PAIR SHARE Why do astronauts need space suits?

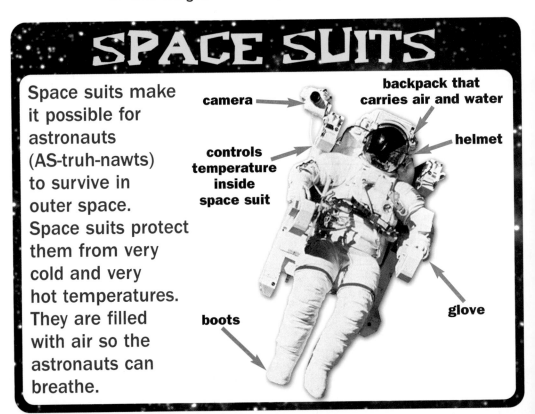

SPACE SUITS

Space suits make it possible for astronauts (AS-truh-nawts) to survive in outer space. Space suits protect them from very cold and very hot temperatures. They are filled with air so the astronauts can breathe.

camera

backpack that carries air and water

controls temperature inside space suit

helmet

glove

boots

Before You Read

Preview the article. Check (✔) the special features it has.

__ title
__ diagram
__ labels
__ pronunciations

As You Read

• Did you read the title?
  ❏ Yes ❏ No

• How many diagrams are in the article?
  ❏ 1 ❏ 2

• Did you read each label?
  ❏ Yes ❏ No

• Explain how you read the diagram.

After You Read

1. What is another word for *breeches*?

2. How are a waistcoat and doublet alike?

PAIR SHARE How were Pilgrim children's clothes like yours? How were they different?

Pilgrim Children

The Pilgrims came to America in 1620. Look at the clothes Pilgrim children wore. The clothes were just like adult clothes. Children began to dress like this at age 6. They wore long sleeves, even in the summer!

hat

waistcoat

apron

petticoat

hat

doublet

breeches

stockings

On Your Own

Below is a diagram of two Native American homes. Think about the facts in this diagram. Remember to:

Step 1 Read the diagram's title and labels.

Step 2 Study the diagram carefully.

Step 3 Think about the information it shows. For example, ask yourself, "What was used to make each home?"

Pawnee Earthlodge

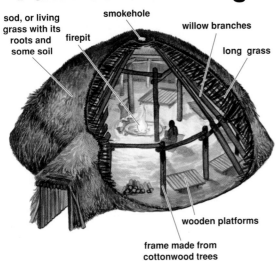

sod, or living grass with its roots and some soil

smokehole

firepit

willow branches

long grass

wooden platforms

frame made from cottonwood trees

Kwakiutl Plankhouse

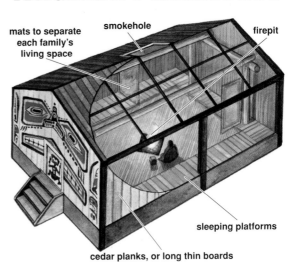

mats to separate each family's living space

smokehole

firepit

sleeping platforms

cedar planks, or long thin boards

Put a ✔ in front of each question that can be answered by the diagram. Then, write another question. When you're done, trade papers with a partner. Answer each other's questions.

❑ **1.** Which home has platforms that are used as beds at night and benches during the day?

❑ **2.** Which home was made of logs cut into long, thin boards?

❑ **3.** Which home has a long, dark tunnel as a doorway?

My Own Question _____

_____

Diagrams

A **diagram** is a special picture that shows the parts of something or how something works. The diagram helps you "picture" the information.

Step 1 Read the title.

It tells you what the diagram is about.
The diagram below shows a nest for ants.

Step 2 Read the captions.
They name parts of the diagram.

Each caption tells about a part of the nest.

Step 3 Follow the numbers.

They help you read the diagram in order.

Practice Your Skills!

1. Underline the title.

2. Circle the label that tells about the queen ant.

3. Put an **X** on the picture of the queen ant.

PAIR SHARE How do the ants work together in their nest?

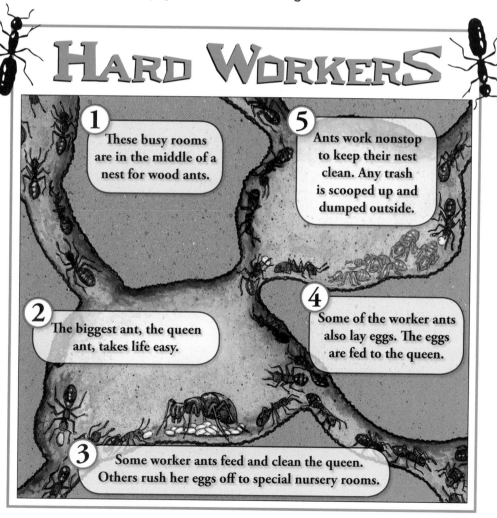

HARD WORKERS

1 These busy rooms are in the middle of a nest for wood ants.

5 Ants work nonstop to keep their nest clean. Any trash is scooped up and dumped outside.

2 The biggest ant, the queen ant, takes life easy.

4 Some of the worker ants also lay eggs. The eggs are fed to the queen.

3 Some worker ants feed and clean the queen. Others rush her eggs off to special nursery rooms.

Before You Read

Preview the article. Check (✔) the special features it has.

__ title
__ diagram
__ labels
__ boldfaced words
__ pronunciations
__ pictures

As You Read

- Did you read each label on the diagram?
  ❏ Yes ❏ No

- Explain how you read the diagram.

After You Read

1. What is a groundhog's home called?

2. What other animals live underground?

PAIR SHARE Why do you think the groundhog's burrow is a good home?

Groundhog Burrow

Parts of a Groundhog Burrow

1 **Main Entrance**
Groundhogs can dig many openings in their burrows.

2 **Tunnels**
The tunnels can be a home for other animals, too. Rabbits and mice sometimes live here. A snake hibernates here. Can you find it?

3 **Sleeping Room**
This is where the groundhog hibernates. It brings in grass to make a soft bed. When it is ready to sleep, it closes this room off with dirt.

4 **Bathroom**
The groundhog uses the end of a tunnel for a bathroom. The groundhog uses this when it is not hibernating.

5 **Back Door**
Big enemies of the groundhog, such as dogs, can't get in.

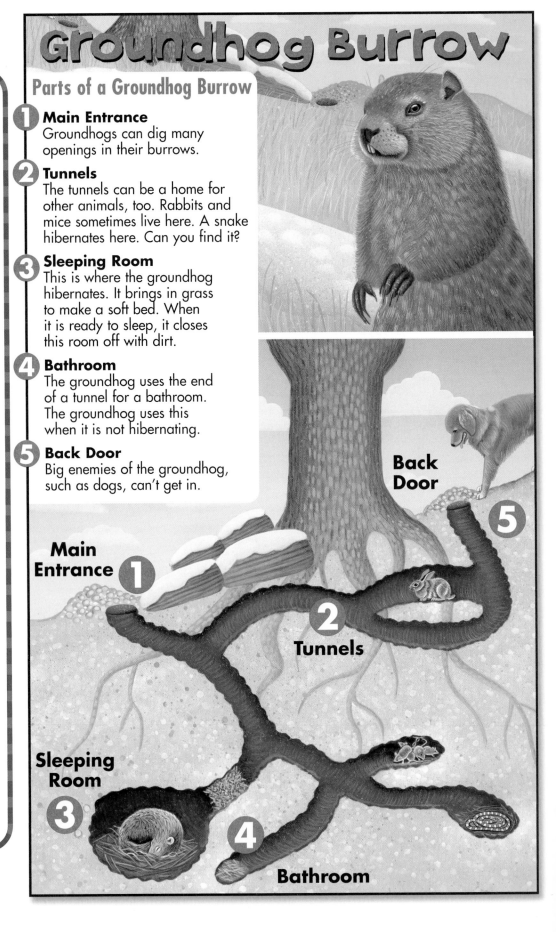

Main Entrance **1**
Back Door **5**
Tunnels **2**
Sleeping Room **3**
4
Bathroom

On Your Own

Here's a diagram of an object you probably see every day—a computer.

 Label the important parts of the computer. Remember to include a line from each label to the part that it names.

 Then add some features to the diagram. Draw and label them.

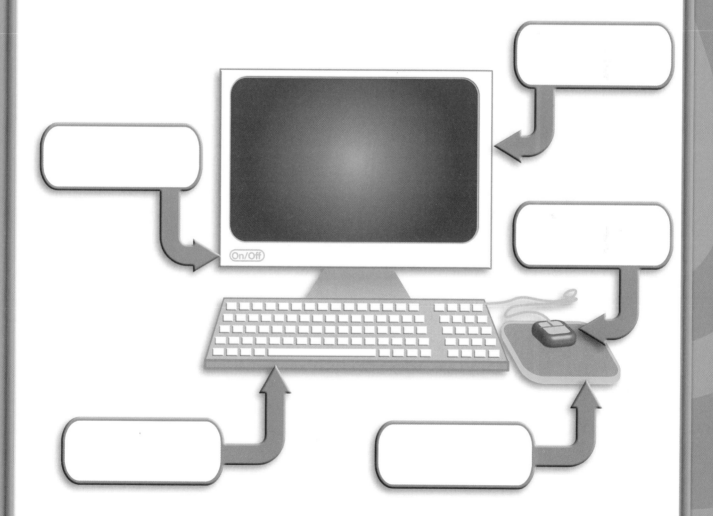

On/Off

 Make a diagram of another common object, such as a telephone, DVD player, or bicycle. Label all the important features of the object.

Description

Before You Read

Vocabulary Tell how the word pairs below are related. Use each pair in a sentence.

Word Connection
crew—ship
masts—sails
bunk—sailors
steered—captain

As You Read

Text Structure The writer of this article **describes** the *Santa Maria,* one of Columbus's boats. As you read, <u>underline</u> sentences that give important details.

Text Feature What did you learn from the diagram?

After You Read

1. Why do you think the author put a map in the article?

2. Use the diagram to tell how many sails were on the *Santa Maria.*

3. Where would you have liked to stay on the ship? Why?

Columbus's Trip

On August 3, 1492, Columbus sailed from Spain. He and a crew, or team, of 40 men sailed on the *Santa Maria.* No one knows exactly what the *Santa Maria* looked like. Historians think the ship may have looked like this diagram. On October 12, 1492, he landed in the Caribbean Islands.

main sail The sails help the ship move.

fore sail

sprit sail

4

Spain

Caribbean Islands

top sail

crow's nest
Sailors can see for miles from the crow's nest.

mast
The masts hold up the sails.

mizzen sail

firebox

bunk

tiller

Life on the Santa Maria

1 Captain's Cabin
Columbus slept, ate, and worked here. As captain of the ship, he was the only one to have his own **bunk**, or bed.

2 Main Deck
Most of the ship's work was done here. One hot meal a day was cooked on the **firebox**, or stove. Pigs, chickens, and other animals were brought on the trip for food.

3 Steerage
The crew steered the ship here. In calm weather, one sailor steered the ship with the **tiller**, or handle. In stormy weather, two or more sailors were needed at the tiller.

4 Hold
Food, water, and supplies were stored here. Water was kept in barrels. Food was given out in small amounts because no one knew how long the trip would take.

Description

Reread "Columbus's Trip." Fill in the graphic organizer to describe the *Santa Maria*.

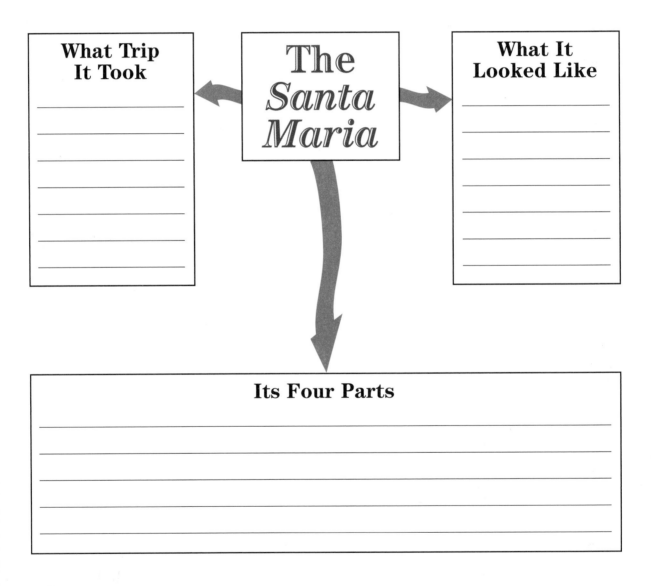

What Trip It Took

_____
_____
_____
_____
_____

The Santa Maria

What It Looked Like

_____
_____
_____
_____
_____

Its Four Parts

_____
_____
_____
_____
_____

 Use the graphic organizer above to help retell "Columbus's Trip" in your own words.

Writing Frame

Use the information in your organizer to fill in the writing frame.

The *Santa Maria* had many interesting features.

One part was the _____.

It was used for _____

_____.

A second part was the _____.

It was used for _____

_____.

A third part was the _____.

It was used for _____

_____.

A fourth part was the _____.

It was used for _____

_____.

 Use the writing frame above as a model to describe another kind of transportation. Look in your social studies textbook if you need more facts to help you fill in the frame.

Text Feature

Flow Charts

A **flow chart** is special kind of picture. It shows the steps in which something happens. Each step is numbered in order. This is how to read a flow chart.

Step 1 **Read the title. It tells you what the flow chart below is about.**
The flow chart shows how jelly is made.

Step 2 **Look at the numbers on the flow chart.**
Start reading at number 1. Then follow the numbers in order.

Step 3 **Look at each photo and read the caption.**
They give you important facts.

Practice Your Skills!

1. Circle the number of the first step.

2. Put an **X** on what happens after the grapes are cooked.

PAIR SHARE Which steps are done by people? Which are done by machines? Why?

From Grapevine to Jelly Jar

① First, a farmer picks the grapes.

② Then, the grapes go to a factory. They are dumped into a machine called a **hopper**. The hopper crushes the grapes.

③ The grapes are cooked in a big pot. They are mixed with sugar and grape juice.

④ Next, a person tastes the grape jelly. She makes sure it is sweet enough.

⑤ Finally, a machine called a **filler** pours the jelly into jars. The jars are shipped to stores.

Before You Read

Preview the article. Check (✔) the special features it has.

__ title
__ photos
__ headings
__ captions
__ numbers
__ labels

As You Read

- Did you read the title of the flow chart?
  ❏ Yes   ❏ No

- Did you read the steps in order?
  ❏ Yes   ❏ No

- Explain how you read the flow chart.

After You Read

1. What are crayons made of?

2. How do crayons get their shape?

PAIR SHARE What is your favorite crayon color?

MAKING CRAYONS

Do you ever wonder where crayons come from? They are made in a **factory**. A factory (FAK-tuh-ree) is a building where things are made in large numbers. Machines usually help make the things. Find out how crayons are made, step by step.

STEP 1
Crayons are made from wax. At the crayon factory, the wax is melted. Then, it is mixed with colored powder.

melted wax
colored powder

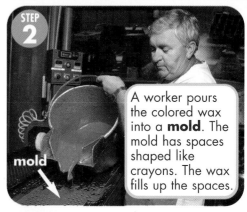

STEP 2
A worker pours the colored wax into a **mold**. The mold has spaces shaped like crayons. The wax fills up the spaces.

mold

STEP 3
The wax dries inside the spaces. A worker turns the mold over. Hard crayons come out!

STEP 4
The crayons go to a machine. The machine puts **labels** on the crayons. The labels say the color of the crayon.

label

crayons

STEP 5
Different colored crayons come together on a moving belt.

moving belt

STEP 6
The belt takes the crayons to boxes. The crayons go in the boxes. Finally, the crayons are ready to go to stores. Time to color!

On Your Own

Make a flow chart. Show how peanuts grow. You can use The Facts to help you. Here's how:

Step 1 Read the flow chart title.

Step 2 Find the number of each step on the flow chart.

Step 3 Use The Facts to write a sentence for each step.

The Facts

A peanut farmer plants seeds in spring. In 10 days, green plants pop up. Yellow flowers bloom four weeks later. In a few months, the peanuts grow under the ground. In the fall, a machine digs up the peanut plants.

HOW PEANUTS GROW

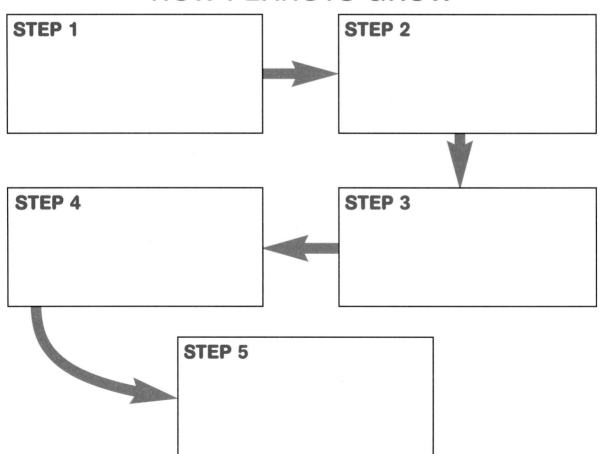

STEP 1

STEP 2

STEP 3

STEP 4

STEP 5

Here's another step for the flow chart: <u>The peanuts are shipped to a factory.</u> There they are made into peanut butter and other foods. Where would you add this step?

Flow Charts

A **flow chart** is special kind of picture. It shows the steps in which something happens. Each step is numbered in order. Follow the steps to read a flow chart.

Step 1 **Read the title. It tells you what the flow chart is about.**

This flow chart shows how a frog grows.

Step 2 **Look at the numbers on the flow chart.**

Start reading at number 1. Then follow the numbers in order. A flow chart may also have arrows to help you.

Step 3 **Look at the photo and read the caption at each step.**

The photo and caption give you important facts.

IT'S A FROG'S LIFE

1 A frog lays its eggs in water.

2 Tadpoles hatch from the eggs. They live in water and breathe through **gills**.

3 Tadpoles begin to grow legs.

4 The tadpoles grow bigger and lose their tails.

5 An adult frog can live on land. It breathes through its **lungs**.

Before You Read

Preview the article. Check (✔) the special features it has.

___ title
___ captions
___ boldfaced words
___ flow chart
___ photos

As You Read

- Did you follow the steps in order?
  ❏ Yes ❏ No

- Explain how you read the flow chart.

After You Read

1. How is the larva's body different from the pupa's?

2. What does a ladybug look like?

PAIR SHARE Why does the flow chart go around in a circle?

How Ladybugs Change and Grow
Ladybugs change a lot over their lives!

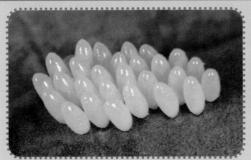

Ladybug Egg

Ladybugs start their lives in an egg. A ladybug mom laid these eggs close together. The eggs were laid on a leaf. They are only as big as the period at the end of this sentence.

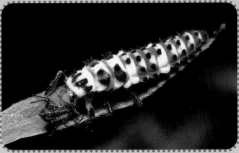

Ladybug Larva

Look what hatched from one of the ladybug eggs! At this stage, it is called a larva. It eats insects called **aphids** (AY-fidz) all day long. Soon its body will change.

Ladybug Pupa

The ladybug larva changed! Now, it is a ladybug pupa (PYOO-puh). The pupa has a hard skin. It sticks to a leaf. Inside its skin, the ladybug is changing one more time.

Ladybug Adult

Now the ladybug is an adult. It will be able to lay eggs and new ladybugs will be born. Can you name the stages the ladybug went through?

A Ladybug's Life Cycle

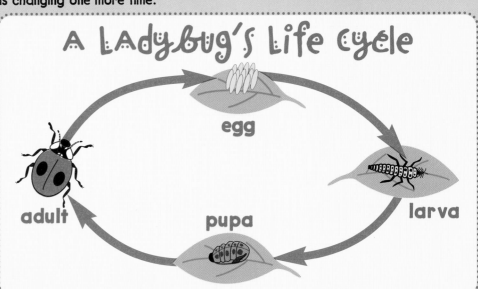

egg

larva

pupa

adult

On Your Own

Make a flow chart. Show the life cycle of a robin. You can use The Facts to help you. Here's how:

Step 1 Give the flow chart a title.

Step 2 Number each step in order.

Step 3 Use The Facts to write a sentence for each step in your flow chart.

The Facts

A robin starts its life as an egg in a nest. A chick grows inside each egg until it gets too big. Then the chick cracks the eggshell and hatches. As the chick grows, it gets new feathers and gets ready to fly. Finally, it is an adult robin.

(Title)

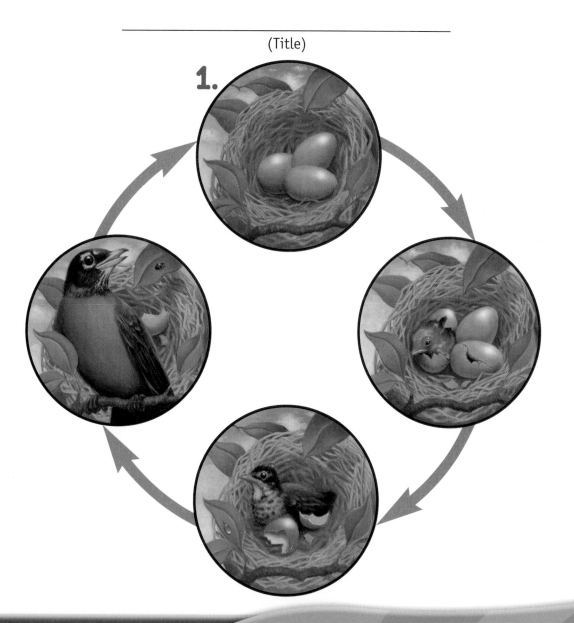

1.

LESSON 12

Sequence

Before You Read

Vocabulary Use the words from the article to fill in the chart.

autumn   energy
caterpillar   nectar

Word	Synonym
fall	
larva	
power	
liquid	

As You Read

Text Structure This article tells the sequence in the butterfly's long trip. Look for clue words, such as *every autumn, at last, then,* and *on the way*. They will help you follow the steps in order. Circle these words in the article.

Text Feature How does the flow chart help you remember the facts in the article?

After You Read

1. Where do monarch butterflies go every autumn?

2. What do you think the butterflies do when winter is over?

3. How is a butterfly's life cycle like a ladybug's? How is it different from a frog's?

TAKE A TRIP, BUTTERFLIES!

It's autumn! The weather is getting colder. Monarch (MON-ark) butterflies need warm weather to live. They fly south, to where it is warm.

Every autumn, monarchs migrate in big flocks, or groups. As they fly south, more and more monarchs join the flock. After all, they are all going to the same places.

On the way, the butterflies stop to drink **nectar**. That's a sweet liquid in flowers. Nectar gives butterflies energy for their long trip south.

At last, the monarchs made it! Some made it all the way to Mexico. Some flew to Florida and California. Now they rest all winter long on trees.

HOW A BUTTERFLY GROWS

Step 1 A butterfly starts its life as an **egg**. The egg is as tiny as this dot. •

Step 2 Then, a **caterpillar** hatches from the egg. The hungry caterpillar eats leaves.

Step 4 Finally, in about two weeks, the chrysalis cracks open. An adult **butterfly** appears!

Step 3 When the caterpillar gets big, it grows a hard skin called a **chrysalis** (KRIS-uh-lis). The caterpillar changes inside as the chrysalis grows.

Sequence

Reread "How a Butterfly Grows." Fill in the graphic organizer to show the life cycle of a monarch butterfly.

A BUTTERFLY'S LIFE

STEP 1

STEP 2

STEP 4

STEP 3

Retell Use the flow chart above to retell "How a Butterfly Grows" in your own words. Remember to tell the steps in the order in which each happens. Think about what happens *first*, *next*, *then*, and *finally*. Include these words in your retelling.

Writing Frame

Use the facts in your graphic organizer to fill in the writing frame.

The first step in a butterfly's life is _____

_____

_____.

Next, _____

_____

_____.

Then, _____

_____

_____.

Finally, _____

_____

_____.

 Use the writing frame above as a model to tell the steps in brushing your teeth.

Captions and Labels

Your science textbook is a treasure chest filled with information. There's the main article plus lots of extra information. This extra information is often a photo with a **caption** and **label**.

How do you read a page with so much stuff on it? Here's how!

Step 1 **Read the title to learn what the article is about.**
The article below is about water.

Step 2 **Read the main article.**
The article gives you the main ideas. The writer wants you to learn and think about rain in the desert.

Step 3 **Look at the photos.**
The photos below show the desert <u>before</u> and <u>after</u> rain.

Step 4 **Read the labels and captions.**
The words **Before** and **After** are labels on the photos. The captions tell what's in each photo.

Practice Your Skills!

1. <u>Underline</u> the title.

2. (Circle) the labels.

3. Put a check (✔) in front of each caption.

PAIR SHARE How are the photos different? What do you learn from them?

✿✿✿ Just Add Water ✿✿✿

Our country has dry deserts. It hardly ever rains in the deserts. When it does rain, some plants and animals spring to life.

Once every few years, it rains a lot in the desert. It rains enough to make seeds in the ground grow quickly. Flowers bloom. All of a sudden, the desert is covered in color! But the flowers won't last long. They only last about two weeks.

Before

Rains wet the ground in the Sonoran Desert in Arizona.

After

After enough rain, the Sonoran Desert blooms with golden poppies.

Before You Read

Preview the article. Check (✔) the special features it has.

___ title
___ photos
___ captions
___ boldfaced word
___ pronunciations
___ labels

As You Read

• Did you read the title?
  ❏ Yes ❏ No

• Did you look carefully at every photo?
  ❏ Yes ❏ No

• What did you learn from the captions and labels?

After You Read

1. What are two ways seed travel?

2. What does **sprout** mean?

PAIR SHARE Why do seeds travel? Why is this important?

Seeds on the Go!

When seeds travel, they move away from their parent plant. Now, they have a chance to find more water and room to **sprout**, or start to grow. Here are some ways seeds get around.

Seeds Spin in Air!

seeds

These two maple seeds fall off the tree and spin in the wind! They work just like a **propeller**. The seeds spin away from the parent tree. Spinning helps the seeds travel farther than if they just fell.

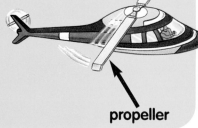

propeller

Seeds Float in Water!

The seed floats.

The seed sprouts.

This coconut is a big seed. It falls from a palm tree into the water. Then, the coconut **floats** like a boat on the water. (A coconut is light enough to float.)

When the coconut gets to a beach, it can sprout into a new palm tree. Coconuts can float to a whole new island (EYE-lind) far away from their parent tree!

On Your Own

Look at a page about seeds that travel on animals. You can make it easier to read. Here's how:

Step 1 Write a title.

Step 2 Add a label to the picture.

Step 3 Write a caption below the picture.

_____
(title)

_____

_____

_____
(caption)

This dog has **burs** on its fur! Tiny hooks all over the burs grab onto animal fur. The animal carries around the burs—and the tiny seeds inside the burs. Sooner or later, the animal scratches off the burs, or they fall to the ground on their own. Either way, the burs get a ride to a new place. Now, the seeds inside the burs can sprout into new plants!

What other things might a bur stick to? Draw a picture on another sheet of paper. Write a caption for your picture.

Captions and Labels

You know that nonfiction gives you information.
Most of the information is in the article. But there
is **added information** in photos, captions, and labels.
This is how to read the page.

Step 1 **Read the title to learn what the article is about.**
The article below tells about Flag Day,
a holiday in the United States.

Step 2 **Read the article.**
The article gives you the main ideas the writer
wants you to learn and think about.

Step 3 **Look at the photos.**
The photos give you more information.
The ones below show the U.S. flag.

Step 4 **Read the label and caption.**
A label names a part of the photo. A caption
tells you about what's in the photo. They both
give you more facts.

Flag Day

JUNE
1 2
3 4 5 6 7 8 9
10 11 12 13 14 15 16
17 18 19 20 21 22 23
24 25 26 27 28 29 30

Flag Day is a holiday that
celebrates our country's flag.
The American flag stands for
all the people of our country
and the freedoms that we care
about. On this holiday, people
carry flags and hang them on
their homes.

13 stripes

Our flag has 50 stars.
Each star stands for
one of the 50 states.

Practice Your Skills!

1. Circle the title.

2. Underline the caption.

3. Make a box around the label.

PAIR SHARE What other caption could you write for the flag?

Chinese New Year

Practice Your Skills!

Before You Read

Preview the article. Check (✔) the special features it has.

__ title
__ photos
__ headings
__ captions
__ map
__ chart
__ labels

As You Read

- Did you read the captions?
  ❏ Yes   ❏ No

- How many labels are on the map?

- How were the labels helpful?

After You Read

1. Is the Los Angeles parade new or old?

2. What did you learn from the captions?

PAIR SHARE What is the difference between the dark and light labels on the map?

Chinese New Year

Happy Chinese New Year! The Chinese New Year is not on the same day every year. It comes in late January or in February. Let's look at how people in the U.S. bring in the New Year, Chinese style.

Maine
Portland
California
Los Angeles

Dragon on Parade

LOS ANGELES, CALIFORNIA

Every year, a dragon comes down the streets of Los Angeles. It's not a real dragon, of course! It is part of the Los Angeles Chinese New Year parade.

The parade always begins with the dragon and firecrackers. Soon, floats, marching bands, drummers, and kung fu performers go by.

Los Angeles has had a Chinese New Year parade every year for 104 years!

Look at Connie spin! She puts her finger in a ring under each handkerchief.

Fun at the Fair

PORTLAND, MAINE

Portland celebrates Chinese New Year with a fair. Children like Connie Yang show their talents. Here, Connie spins handkerchiefs on her fingers. "It's traditional," she says. "I learned how in China." Connie lived in China before her family moved to Maine.

This year, people at the fair will learn about Chinese culture. They will also play games and eat a Chinese lunch.

On Your Own

Look at this page about another Chinese New Year celebration. You can make it easier to read. Here's how:

Step 1 Write a title.

Step 2 Add a label to the picture.

Step 3 Write a caption below the picture.

(title)

This family lives in Chicago. The family has a feast at home for Chinese New Year. Many other families across the country do too. People prepare the feast before the New Year begins. It's supposed to be bad luck to cook on Chinese New Year. This family uses chopsticks to enjoy duck, dumplings, and fish. Yum!

(caption)

Write three questions that could be answered by the article. Use the words such as those in the list. When you're done, trade papers with a partner. Answer each other's questions.

What
Where
When
Which

1. _____

_____

2. _____

_____

3. _____

_____

Cause/Effect

Practice Your Skills!

Before You Read

Vocabulary Use the words to fill in the circles.

chameleon

reservoir   violet

As You Read

Text Structure The writer of this article tells the **effects** of rain on plants and animals. Underline the sentences that tell the effects of rain.

Text Feature How do the labels help you understand the article?

After You Read

1. What effect does rain have on plants? on animals?

2. What might happen if a reservoir becomes empty?

3. How can clouds help you predict weather? What clouds do you see today?

Amazing

roots

RAIN MAKES PLANTS GROW

Plants need water to live. First, rainwater sinks into the ground. Then, plants suck up the water with their roots. The plants use the water to make food for themselves. The food helps them grow and grow!

Each rainbow has seven colors—red, orange, yellow, green, blue, indigo, and violet!

RAIN MAKES A RAINBOW

After it rains, there are still some tiny drops of water in the air. The drops are so tiny that we can't see them. When the sun shines through those drops, it makes different colors. The colors from all the drops make a rainbow!

Rain

People can get a drink from rain, too! People store water in special places called **reservoirs** (REZ-er-vwarz). Rain fills up the reservoirs. Then, water from the reservoirs is cleaned. It travels to our homes in pipes. That's the water you use every day!

reservoir

chameleon drinking

RAIN GIVES EVERYONE A DRINK!

Rain gives thirsty animals a drink. Some animals drink rainwater from puddles on the ground. Others drink raindrops right off plants!

HOW TO TELL IF IT WILL RAIN
Sometimes you can tell if it is going to rain by looking at clouds!

cumulus

If you see clouds like this, then it probably will <u>not</u> rain.

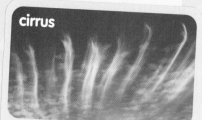
cirrus

If you see clouds like this, then it might rain tomorrow.

stratus

If you see clouds like this, then it might rain a little today.

cumulonimbus

If you see clouds like this, then it might rain a lot today! Bring an umbrella!

Cause/Effect

Reread "Amazing Rain." Fill in the chart to show what happens when it rains.

Cause	Effects
Rain goes into the ground.	Plants _____ _____ _____ _____ _____ .
Rain makes puddles on the ground.	Animals _____ _____ _____ _____ _____ .
Rain fills reservoirs.	People _____ _____ _____ _____ _____ .

Retell Use the graphic organizer above to retell "Amazing Rain" in your own words. Remember to include the effects that no rain would have on plants, animals, and people.

Writing Frame

Use the information in your graphic organizer to fill in the writing frame.

All living things need water. Plants need water to _____

_____.

If plants had no water, then _____

_____.

Animals need water because _____

_____.

If animals had no water, then _____

_____.

People need water because _____

_____.

If people had no water, then _____

_____.

 Use the writing frame above as a model to tell the effects of plants on people and animals. Begin with the sentence, "People and animals need plants."

Text Feature

Headings

Many books and articles show information in a way that tells you the main ideas. Writers of these books and articles put in clues to help you as you read.

- The **title** tells what the article is about. This is the topic of the *whole* article.

- **Headings** give the main ideas for each section of the text. Headings often are shown in special type, such as CAPITAL LETTERS, a different color, or **boldfaced**.

- **Details** are the facts about each main idea in the text. Under each heading, you will find text containing these details.

Practice Your Skills!

1. Draw a box around the title.

2. Circle the heading.

3. Underline two sentences that give important details.

PAIR SHARE Why is a baby carrier an important invention?

baby carrier

Women Inventors

A New Baby Carrier

Some inventions solve problems. A woman named Ann Moore knew it was hard to do things while holding a baby. So, in 1965, she invented a new kind of baby carrier. This helps people carry their babies without using their hands. Problem solved!

Practice Your Skills!

Before You Read

Preview the article. Check (✔) the special features it has.

__ graph
__ headings
__ photos
__ boldfaced words
__ diagrams
__ labels

As You Read

- Did you read the title?
  ❏ Yes   ❏ No

- Did you read the headings to learn the main ideas?
  ❏ Yes   ❏ No

- How did the headings help you remember the facts in this article?

After You Read

1. How are these two scientists alike? different?

2. What measures temperature?

PAIR SHARE How have these scientists helped solve problems?

Women Scientists of Today

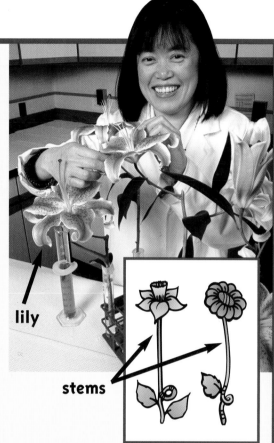

lily

stems

Learning About Plants

Susan Han studies plants. She learns how to keep flower **stems** and leaves green after the flowers are cut. She also learns how to make flowers, like lilies, as bright as they can be.

temperature 20°

Learning About the Ocean

Monica Stevens studies the ocean. She finds out the **temperature** of the ocean in different places. Then, she creates pictures of the ocean's temperatures on a computer.

On Your Own

Make a chart about you! Here's how:

Step 1 Give the chart a title.
Your name can be the title.

Step 2 Write the main idea in the
big box. This is a sentence
that best describes you.

Step 3 Answer some of the questions
below about yourself. Put your
answers in the "Detail" boxes.

- When is your birthday?
- Who is in your family?
- What do you look like?
- How old are you?
- What subjects and hobbies do you like?
- What else would you like to share about yourself?

Main Idea

Detail

Detail

Detail

Text Feature

Headings

Many books and articles show information in a way that tells you the main ideas. Writers of these books and articles put in clues to help you as you read.

Step 1 **Read the title to find out what the article is about.**

The title tells us that this article is about spiders.

Step 2 **Read the heading to find out the main idea.**

The heading tells us that we will learn about spider silk.

Step 3 **Look for details to get more facts.**

Under the heading are sentences that give more facts.

Practice Your Skills!

1. Put an **X** on the title.

2. Circle the heading.

PAIR SHARE Tell two ways spider silk is used.

Those Amazing Spiders

Spider Silk

People are finding ways to use spider silk for the things they need. Spider silk is super strong. It stretches, too. So scientists like Randy Lewis want to use it in new ways. "Spider silk could be used to make ropes, seat belts, and clothes for firefighters," says Dr. Lewis.

Spiders don't make enough silk for people to use, though. Dr. Lewis is finding out how people can make silk like spiders do.

Dr. Lewis shows his spider to a class of second and third graders.

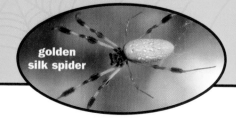

golden silk spider

Before You Read

Preview the article. Check (✔) the special features it has.

__ title
__ introduction
__ headings
__ boldfaced words
__ pronunciations
__ photos

As You Read

- Did you read the headings to learn the main ideas?
  ❏ Yes ❏ No

- Circle a detail under each heading.

- Explain how the headings helped you remember the facts in the article.

After You Read

1. What helps some animals stay warm?

2. How does a woodpecker get food?

PAIR SHARE What body parts help you with food, water, and temperature?

How Animals' Body Parts Help Them Survive

Some animals have body parts that help them meet their needs—food, water, and the right body temperature.

Food

Many animals have special mouth or head parts that help them get food. For example, this woodpecker uses its long beak to get under a tree's bark. Then it can eat the bugs that live there.

Water

Some animals have special body parts that help them get water. The camel, for example, does not **sweat** (SWET) much, even in desert heat. This is because it saves water in its **tissues**, which are cells that form part of the body. That is why a camel can go without drinking for nearly a month.

Temperature

Some animals have long coats that keep them warm in cold temperatures. The **yak** lives high in the mountains in Tibet (tuh-BET), a country in Asia. It needs its woolly coat to keep warm.

On Your Own

Read the chart below. Use the chart to write a paragraph about what you learned. You can add more information if you wish.

Land Care

Main Idea
People can take care of our land.

Detail
We plant trees for animal homes and to keep soil from blowing away.

Detail
We pick up litter and put it in trash cans.

Detail
We make less trash by using old things again.

Detail
We make less trash by recycling, or using old things to make new things. We recycle paper, for example.

 Write what you learned.

_____

_____

_____

_____

_____

Problem/Solution

Before You Read

Vocabulary Use these and other words to finish the web.

rescue   robot   tools

Who?   Why?

⟨ ⟩   ⟨ ⟩

⟨ firefighting ⟩

⟨ ⟩

With What?

As You Read

Text Structure The author of this article explains a **problem** and some **solutions**. As you read, circle each solution.

Text Features Notice that a title and headings may give solutions. What problem does the writer discuss? What are some solutions?

After You Read

1. Which cool tools did you know about before reading? Which did you learn about?

2. Why is *cool* an interesting way to describe fire tools?

3. Why is a firefighter's job hard?

TODAY'S COOL FIRE TOOLS

ROCKVILLE E-32 VOLUNTEERS

Fighting fires is difficult. How do firefighters put out fires? They use **tools**. You've probably seen firefighters use hoses and fire trucks. They have other important tools, too.

FIRE SHELTERS BEAT THE HEAT

Firefighters can put out forest fires from the ground. When the fire gets too close, they can go inside a **fire shelter**. The shelter keeps them safe from heat.

ROBOT TO THE RESCUE

Urbie is a new **robot**. Urbie will probably be ready to go into burning buildings soon.

Inside, Urbie will search for people with its camera eyes. It will let firefighters know where the people are. Then, firefighters can save the people.

FIREFIGHTERS ARE HEROES

Firefighters use many cool tools to do their jobs. Still, they must get close to dangerous fires. They are **brave**. Firefighters save people's homes and lives. They save animals, too. Thanks, firefighters!

Problem/Solution

Reread "Today's Cool Fire Tools." Fill in the graphic organizer.

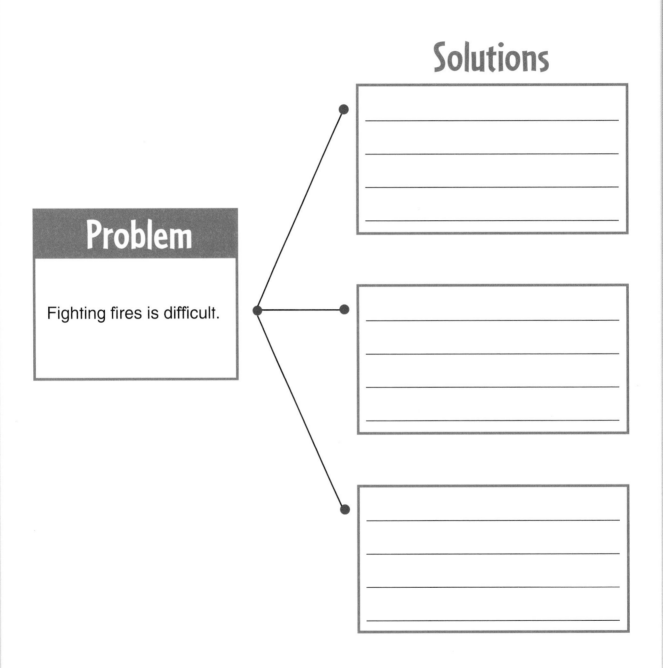

Solutions

Problem

Fighting fires is difficult.

Retell Use the graphic organizer above to retell "Today's Cool Fire Tools" in your own words. Remember to start with the problem and include the different solutions.

Writing Frame

Use the information in your graphic organizer to fill in the writing frame.

Fighting fires is difficult. There are many ways firefighters solve this problem.

One way to solve the problem is to _____

_____

_____.

Another way to solve the problem is to _____

_____

_____.

Finally, _____

_____

_____

_____.

Firefighters are brave people!

 Use the writing frame above as a model to explain how to be safe from fire at home or in school. Look in your social studies textbook if you need facts that will help you fill in the frame.

Maps

A map is a flat picture of Earth. A map shows where places are. It gives a lot of information in a small space. That's why a map often uses symbols instead of words. Follow the steps to read a map.

Step 1 Read the map title.

It tells you what the map is about.
The map below is a weather map.

Step 2 Find the map symbols.

A symbol stands for a real thing or place.
It may be a picture (⭐) or a special color.

Step 3 Look at the map key.

It tells what each symbol means.

Step 4 Read the map labels.

The labels on the map below name cities.

Step 5 Find the compass rose.

It shows directions on a map. **N** stands for north, **S** stands for south, **E** stands for east, and **W** stands for west.

Weather Watch

A weather map shows the weather in different places.

Practice Your Skills!

1. Underline the map title.

2. Circle the map key.

3. What is the symbol for a warm, sunny day? Why?

PAIR SHARE What is the weather in Dallas, Texas? How did you figure it out?

Before You Read

Preview the article. Check (✔) the special features it has.

___ title
___ map
___ photos
___ labels
___ diagram
___ chart

As You Read

- What is the Weather Wheel?
  ❏ photo
  ❏ diagram

- What does the symbol ★ mean?
  ❏ state
  ❏ capital city

- Tell how you read the map.

After You Read

1. What is the weather like in Florida?

2. How did the map key help you?

PAIR SHARE Describe the weather where you live.

Weather in Our Country

What kind of weather does your community have?

The weather wheel, to the right, shows words that describe weather.

Which words describe your community's weather?

Think about the weather where you live. What do you enjoy doing in the winter? How do you have fun in the summer?

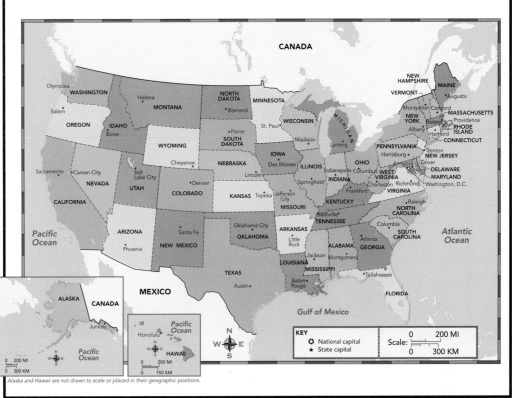

Rainy Sunny Cold

Cool **Weather Wheel** Warm

Damp Snowy

Hot Cloudy Dry

KEY
✪ National capital
★ State capital

Scale: 0 — 200 MI
0 — 300 KM

Alaska and Hawaii are not drawn to scale or placed in their geographic positions.

On Your Own

Look at the map on this page. You can make it easier to read.

Step 1 Read The Facts.

Step 2 Complete the Map Key.
- Add the symbol for a state capital.
- Add the symbol for a city.
- Color in each raindrop with a different color.

Step 3 Update the map using the Map Key.

The Facts

- Washington is in the northwestern United States. It is the only state named after a president.
- Western Washington has cool summers and mild winters but heavy rain. Seattle gets almost 35 inches of rain a year.
- Eastern Washington has hot summers and cold winters, but it is much drier. There are up to 28 inches of rain each year in northeastern Washington. Spokane gets about 17 inches of rain. Walla Walla gets about 15 inches.

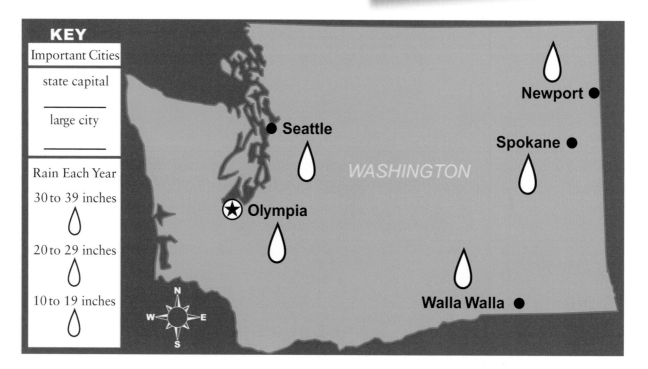

KEY

Important Cities

state capital

_____

large city

_____

Rain Each Year

30 to 39 inches

20 to 29 inches

10 to 19 inches

Newport ●

Seattle ●

WASHINGTON

Spokane ●

⭐ Olympia

Walla Walla ●

What is the rainfall like in your city throughout the year? How can you find out how much rain falls? Compare your rainfall to the amount of rain in Washington's cities.

Maps

A **map** is a flat picture of Earth. A map shows where places are. It gives a lot of information in a small space. That's why a map often has symbols instead of words.

Step 1 Read the map title.

It tells you what the map is about.

Step 2 Find the map symbols.

A symbol stands for a real thing or place. It may be a picture (⭐) or a special **color**. The map below uses color.

Step 3 Look at the map key.

It tells what each symbol means.

Step 4 Read the map labels.

The labels on the map below name states.

Step 5 Find the compass rose.

It show directions on a map. **N** stands for north, **S** for south, **E** for east, and **W** for west.

Practice Your Skills!

1. Underline the title of the map.

2. Put an **X** on a state with many fires.

3. Put a ★ on a state with few fires.

PAIR SHARE Why do you think some places have more fires in the summer?

Helicopters Help Out!

Every summer, forests in the western part of our country are hot and dry. Big forest fires can happen. That's when fire **helicopters** fly in. The pilots drop water from the air and put those fires out!

U.S. States With the Most Forest Fires

Washington
Montana
Oregon
Idaho
Nevada
Utah
Colorado
California
Arizona
New Mexico
Texas

Alaska*

* **NOTE:** Alaska is not in place and not drawn to scale.

North
West — East
South

Map Key
▮ many forest fires
▯ few forest fires

My Dad Is a Park Ranger

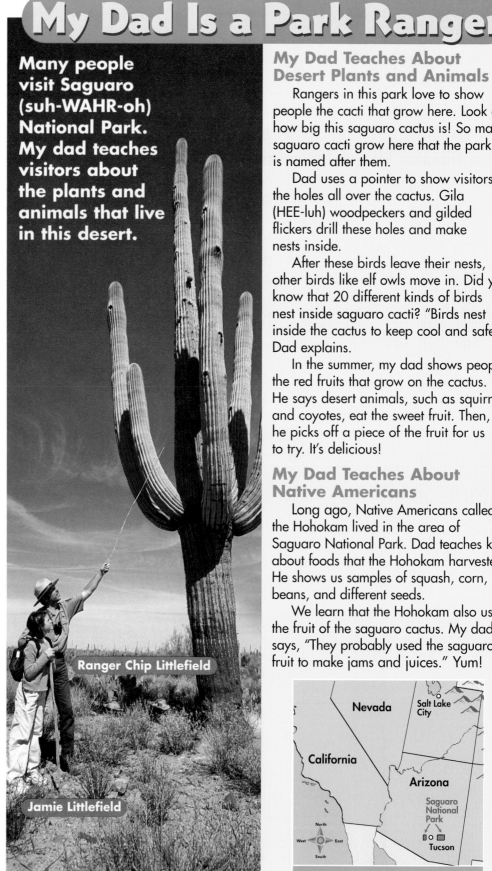

Many people visit Saguaro (suh-WAHR-oh) National Park. My dad teaches visitors about the plants and animals that live in this desert.

Ranger Chip Littlefield

Jamie Littlefield

My Dad Teaches About Desert Plants and Animals

Rangers in this park love to show people the cacti that grow here. Look at how big this saguaro cactus is! So many saguaro cacti grow here that the park is named after them.

Dad uses a pointer to show visitors the holes all over the cactus. Gila (HEE-luh) woodpeckers and gilded flickers drill these holes and make nests inside.

After these birds leave their nests, other birds like elf owls move in. Did you know that 20 different kinds of birds nest inside saguaro cacti? "Birds nest inside the cactus to keep cool and safe," Dad explains.

In the summer, my dad shows people the red fruits that grow on the cactus. He says desert animals, such as squirrels and coyotes, eat the sweet fruit. Then, he picks off a piece of the fruit for us to try. It's delicious!

My Dad Teaches About Native Americans

Long ago, Native Americans called the Hohokam lived in the area of Saguaro National Park. Dad teaches kids about foods that the Hohokam harvested. He shows us samples of squash, corn, beans, and different seeds.

We learn that the Hohokam also used the fruit of the saguaro cactus. My dad says, "They probably used the saguaro fruit to make jams and juices." Yum!

Nevada

Salt Lake City

California

Arizona

Saguaro National Park

North
West • East
South

Tucson

MAP KEY
○ = city   ▭ = park land

On Your Own

Think of your classroom as a flat picture. Now make a map of it.

Draw the shape of your classroom below. Leave spaces where doors and windows are. Add desks, tables, and symbols for other things. Remember to:

Step 1 Write a title for the map.

Step 2 Add labels.

Step 3 Make a map key to explain the symbols you use.

_____

Write three questions that could be answered by your map. Use words such as those in the list. When you're done, trade papers with a partner. Answer each other's questions.

What
Where
How

1. _____
   _____

2. _____
   _____

3. _____
   _____

Text Structure

Description

BE A DINO DETECTIVE

Before You Read

Vocabulary Use these words to fill in the web.

carnivore   fossils

triceratops   T. rex

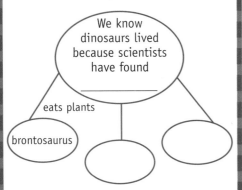

We know dinosaurs lived because scientists have found _____

eats plants

brontosaurus

As You Read

Text Structure The writer of this article **describes** a famous dinosaur discovery. As you read, underline words that give important details.

Text Feature What facts did you learn from the map? How does the map go with the article?

After You Read

1. Why are fossils useful?

2. Tell four details, or facts, about the T. rex.

3. Use the map to tell in what part of the U.S. the T. rexes lived.

Clue:
Dinosaur Sue has short arms for such a big body. Each arm is about the size of a human arm.

What it might mean:
Nobody knows why her arms are so short. How do you think Sue used her short arms?

Clue:
Dinosaur Sue has sharp, pointy teeth.

What it might mean:
T. rexes were **carnivores**, or meat eaters. They probably hunted other dinosaurs, like the **triceratops** (try-SAIR-uh-tops). Scientists think T. rexes also ate turtles because they found a turtle fossil near Dinosaur Sue's fossil.

Sue Hendrickson found Dinosaur Sue's fossil in South Dakota. Her dog is named Skywalker.

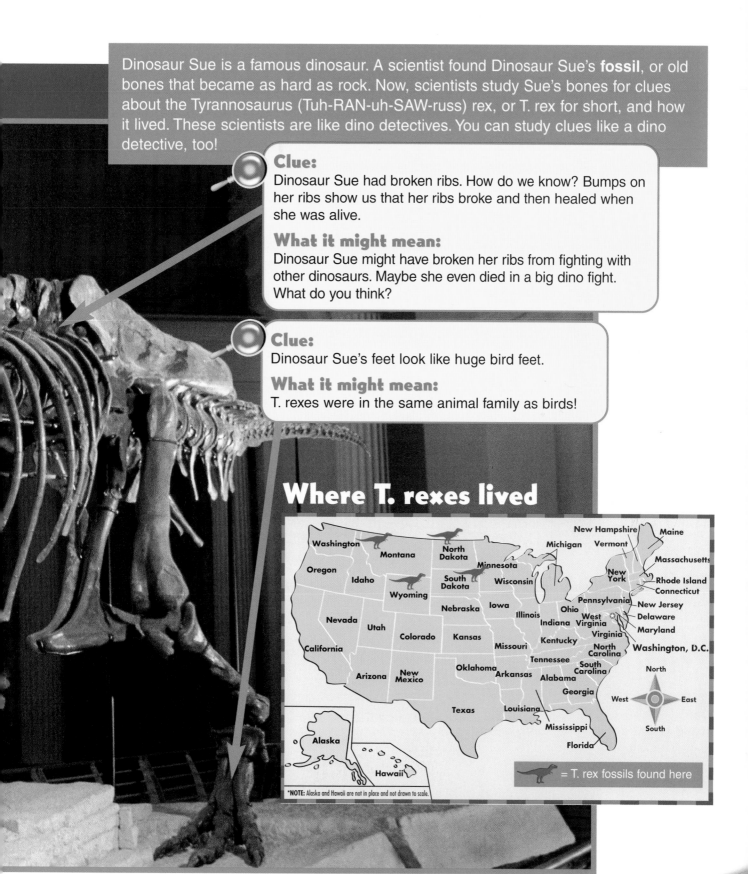

Dinosaur Sue is a famous dinosaur. A scientist found Dinosaur Sue's **fossil**, or old bones that became as hard as rock. Now, scientists study Sue's bones for clues about the Tyrannosaurus (Tuh-RAN-uh-SAW-russ) rex, or T. rex for short, and how it lived. These scientists are like dino detectives. You can study clues like a dino detective, too!

Clue:
Dinosaur Sue had broken ribs. How do we know? Bumps on her ribs show us that her ribs broke and then healed when she was alive.

What it might mean:
Dinosaur Sue might have broken her ribs from fighting with other dinosaurs. Maybe she even died in a big dino fight. What do you think?

Clue:
Dinosaur Sue's feet look like huge bird feet.

What it might mean:
T. rexes were in the same animal family as birds!

Where T. rexes lived

Washington
Oregon
Montana
North Dakota
Minnesota
Michigan
New Hampshire
Maine
Vermont
Massachusetts
New York
Rhode Island
Connecticut
Idaho
Wyoming
South Dakota
Wisconsin
Pennsylvania
New Jersey
Nevada
Utah
Nebraska
Iowa
Illinois
Indiana
Ohio
West Virginia
Delaware
Maryland
California
Colorado
Kansas
Missouri
Kentucky
Virginia
North Carolina
Washington, D.C.
Arizona
New Mexico
Oklahoma
Arkansas
Tennessee
South Carolina
Alabama
Georgia
North
Texas
Louisiana
West
East
Mississippi
South
Florida
Alaska
Hawaii

= T. rex fossils found here

*NOTE: Alaska and Hawaii are not in place and not drawn to scale.

Description

Reread "Be a Dino Detective." Fill in the fact card to show what you learned about the T. rex from each clue. Draw a picture in the box.

4 Fast Facts

T. rex

1. _____

2. _____

3. _____

4. _____

 Use the fact card above to retell "Be a Dino Detective" in your own words.

Writing Frame

Use the information in your fact card to fill in the writing frame.

We can tell a lot about a T. rex by looking at its features.

First, _____.

This means _____

_____.

Second, _____.

This means _____

_____.

Third, _____.

This means _____.

Last, _____.

This means _____

_____.

 Use the writing frame above as a model to describe another animal. Look in your science textbook if you need more facts to help you fill in the frame.

Text Feature

Charts

A **chart** shows facts about a topic in a simple way. For example, a chart may show pictures of different trees and labels telling what foods grow on the trees. The chart helps you "picture" the information. It also makes it easy for you to compare and contrast the facts.

Step 1 **Read the title to find out what the chart shows.**
The chart below shows that chocolate comes from trees.

Step 2 **Read the headings on the columns.**
Columns go up and down. Start reading at the top of each column. The chart below shows only one column, which is one part of a bigger chart.

Step 3 **Read the information in each part of the chart.**
Study the pictures. Read the text. Both give you important facts.

Chocolate Comes From Trees

Did you know that chocolate comes from trees? First, people pick beans from the **cacao** (kuh-KAY-oh) tree. Then, people bake the beans, grind them, and mix them with milk and sugar. That makes chocolate! What's your favorite chocolate treat?

cacao tree

The beans grow inside these pods.

chocolate

Before You Read

Preview the article. Check (✔) the special features it has.

__ title
__ photos
__ headings
__ captions
__ chart
__ labels

As You Read

- Did you read the article title?
  ❏ Yes ❏ No

- Did you read the headings on the chart?
  ❏ Yes ❏ No

- How many trees are on the chart?
  ❏ 2 ❏ 3

- Explain how you read the chart.

After You Read

1. What comes from trees?

2. How is paper made?

PAIR SHARE What comes from trees where you live?

What Comes From Trees?

Furniture Comes From Trees

People carve wood to make tables, chairs, beds, and bookcases. Can you find furniture made of wood in your classroom?

Paper Comes From Trees

A machine cuts wood into chips. The chips soak until they turn into mush. Another machine presses the mush into sheets. When the sheets dry, they become paper.

Rubber Comes From Trees

When this woman cuts the rubber tree, white liquid runs into a cup. She brings the rubber to a factory. People turn the liquid into rubber bands, erasers, and balloons!

Tree	What Is Made From It?
 white oak tree	furniture
 white pine tree	papers
 rubber tree	 rubber bands, balloons, erasers

On Your Own

Use The Facts to finish the chart.
Add other facts you know.

Fruit Comes From Trees	
Kind of Tree	**How Its Fruit Is Used**
apple tree	
orange tree	
peach tree	

 Add another row to the chart. Use your social studies textbook for help. You can draw pictures, too.

LESSON 23

Text Feature

Charts

A **chart** shows facts about a topic in a simple way. The chart helps you "picture" the information. It also makes it easy for you to compare and contrast the facts.

Step 1 **Read the title to find out what the chart shows.** The chart below shows different forms of water.

Step 2 **Read the headings on the columns.** Columns go up and down. The headings at the top of each column and the picture labels explain what you are looking at. The chart below shows only one column, which is one part of a bigger chart that you will see later.

Step 3 **Read the information in each part of the chart.** Study the pictures. Read the captions. Both give you important facts.

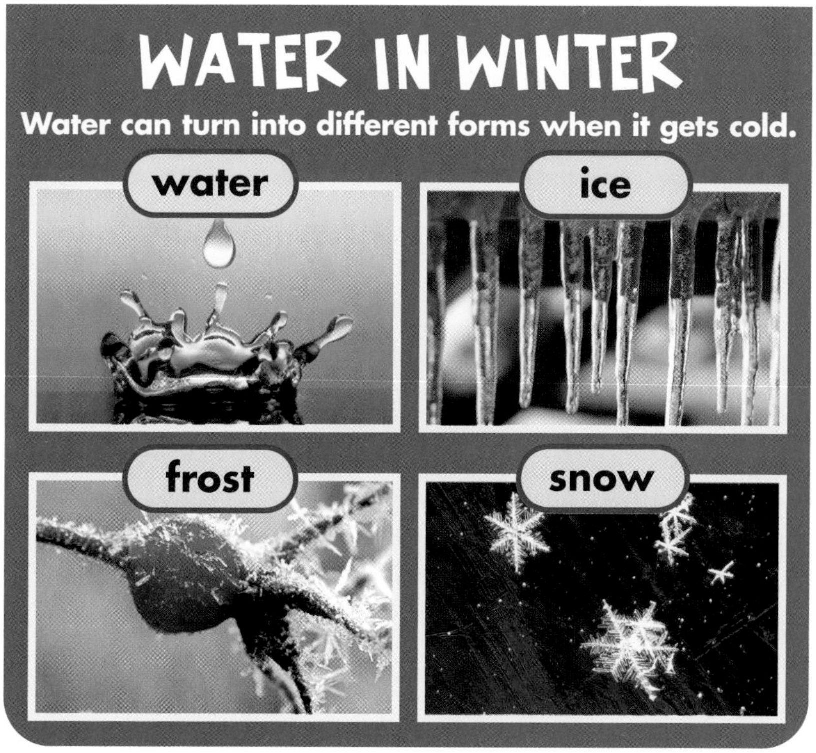
WATER IN WINTER
Water can turn into different forms when it gets cold.
water
ice
frost
snow

Practice Your Skills!

1. Circle the title.

2. How many forms of water are on the chart?

PAIR SHARE Which forms of water can you now see where you live?

Weather is powerful! It can help *and* harm all living things.

 HELPFUL

 HARMFUL

 WIND

dandelion seeds

Wind helps spread seeds. Just look at this dandelion. The wind lifts the dandelion (DAN-duh-lie-un) seeds like parachutes. Then, it takes them to new places where they can sprout into plants.

funnel

thundercloud

Wind can make a dangerous storm. A tornado (tor-NAY-doe) is a spinning storm. Its winds are strong. A tornado forms when air spins under a thundercloud. The air whirls around and around. It stretches to the ground in a **funnel** shape. Then, it rips up everything in its path!

 SUN

solar panel

The sun helps warm some houses. Special **solar panels** on the roof trap the sun's heat. This heat can be used to warm the home's air and water. Heating a home this way is good for the environment.

The sun can also cause a sunburn. Ouch! Here are three ways to stay safe in the sun:
1. Wear sunscreen.
2. Wear a hat.
3. Play in the shade!

On Your Own

Helpful or Harmful?

Look at each picture. Decide if it shows helpful or harmful weather. Put a ✔ in the correct box to fill in the chart. Then, write why the weather in each picture is helpful or harmful.

	Helpful Weather	Harmful Weather	Why?

Write three questions the chart could answer. Use words such as those in the list.
When you're done, trade papers with a partner.
Answer each other's questions.

Why
When
How

1. _____

_____

2. _____

_____

3. _____

_____

Compare/Contrast

Before You Read

Vocabulary Read these words from the article. Use them to fill in the chart. Then add other words to each box.

position   president
elected   office

Person	Action	Thing

As You Read

Text Structure The writer of this article **compares and contrasts** two men who became president of the U.S. As you read, circle words that tell how things are different, such as *unlike*, *but*, and *however*.

Text Feature The writer uses a chart to help you compare and contrast facts.

After You Read

1. Who do we remember on Presidents' Day?

2. How are a king and a president alike? different?

3. How were Washington and Lincoln alike? different?

Before They Were Presidents

Meet **George Washington** and **Abraham Lincoln.** They were two of the most important presidents in our country's history. Before they were presidents, they were children!

George Washington
1732–1799

Abraham Lincoln
1809–1865

George Washington was born in Virginia. Young George lived in a house on a farm. He had a big family. There were five children! The children helped their parents by carrying water to drink from a stream.

Until **George** was 11, he didn't go to school. His mother taught the children in their home. George and his sister had lessons together. They practiced writing on small boards called **slates**.

Unlike George, **Abraham Lincoln** was born in Kentucky. Young Abe lived in a log cabin on a farm. He had one big sister. Like George, Abe and his sister helped their parents. They chopped wood and fed the farm animals.

Abraham went to school but not for very long. He read every book he could find, though! He read in the house and outside on the farm. One of his favorite books was about George Washington!

When the boys grew up, they each made their mark on history. **George Washington** became our 1st president. **Abraham Lincoln** became president, too. He was our 16th president. We remember them both on Presidents' Day!

Did You Know?
Abraham was born almost 100 years after **George**. They did not live at the same time.

No King for U.S.

King	President
Born into the position	Elected by the people
Works alone to make decisions	Works with others to make decisions
Cannot be voted out of office	Can be voted out of office
Has the job for life	Elected to a four-year term

Compare/Contrast

Reread "Before They Were Presidents." Then fill in the organizer. Show how George Washington and Abraham Lincoln were similar, yet different.

	George Washington	Abe Lincoln
state where born		
home		
brothers and sisters		
helped parents by		
schooling		
which president (number)		

 Use the graphic organizer above to retell "Before They Were Presidents" in your own words. Remember to include ways Washington and Lincoln were alike and different.

Writing Frame

Use the information in your graphic organizer to fill in the writing frame.

Both George Washington and Abraham Lincoln were the same in some ways.

They were the same because they both _____

_____

_____.

In some ways, though, George Washington and Abraham Lincoln

were different.

They were different because _____

_____

_____.

So, George Washington and Abraham Lincoln were the same in some

ways and different in other ways.

Use the writing frame above as a model to compare and contrast two other people, such as two other presidents or two famous Americans. Look in your social studies textbook if you need more facts to help you fill in the frame.

Text Feature

Graphs

A **bar graph** is a special kind of picture. It shows the amounts, or numbers, of things at a glance. Each bar on the graph stands for one amount.

Step 1 Read the title.

The bar graph below shows how students voted for a class pet.

Step 2 Read the labels on the bar graph.

The labels on the bottom are **words**. They tell **what** pets the graph is about. The labels on the side are **numbers**. They show **how many** students voted.

Step 3 Find the information that each bar gives.

Move your finger from the bottom of the bar to the top. Then read the number on the left side.

Step 4 Compare and contrast the information on the graph.

For example, figure out which pet got the most votes. How many voted for a snake?

Practice Your Skills!

1. Color in the bar that shows which pet got the most votes.

2. Circle the two animal names that got the same number of votes.

3. How many votes did the hamster get?

PAIR SHARE Which pet would you vote for? Why?

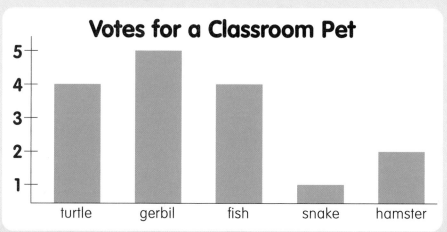

Let's Vote!

Voting is a way people can pick what they want. When you vote, the person or thing that gets the most votes is the winner. This is called **majority rule**, what the largest number of voters want.

Votes for a Classroom Pet

	5	4	3	2	1
turtle		4			
gerbil	5				
fish		4			
snake					1
hamster				2	

MEET GARY SOTO

Gary Soto is a Mexican-American author who writes about growing up in California. Here is an interview with Gary Soto.

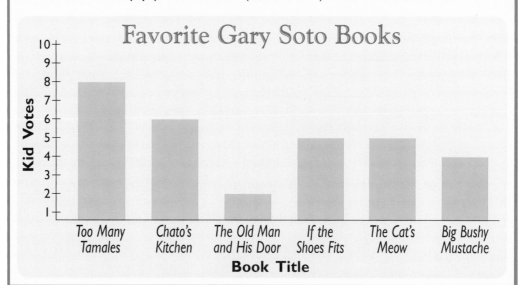

Gary Soto reads his book _Too Many Tamales_ to some friends.

QUESTION: **What do you like to write about?**

ANSWER: Childhood memories, both funny and **tragic**, or sad. I write about what happened in the past, not what is happening now.

QUESTION: **What is it like to speak two languages?**

ANSWER: Knowing two languages helps you to know more about the world. To dream in two languages is very cool.

QUESTION: **What advice do you have for kids about writing?**

ANSWER: Books are beautiful to hold and beautiful to read. Start your own library and read as much as you can. As for writing, don't worry about doing it well the first time. Just play and enjoy. _¡Buena suerte!_ (Good luck!)

Favorite Gary Soto Books

Kid Votes

Book	Votes
Too Many Tamales	8
Chato's Kitchen	6
The Old Man and His Door	2
If the Shoes Fits	5
The Cat's Meow	5
Big Bushy Mustache	4

Book Title

On Your Own

Make a bar graph. Show how many students in Mr. Katz's class play instruments. You can use The Facts to help you. Here's how:

The Facts

In Mr. Katz's class,
7 children play the piano,
4 children play the violin,
2 children play the drums,
1 child plays the recorder,
and 2 children play
the guitar.

Step 1 Read the bar graph title and labels.

Step 2 Write the names of the instruments on the lines at the bottom of the graph.

Step 3 Use The Facts to make the bars on your graph.

Instruments We Play

Number of Kids

8
7
6
5
4
3
2
1

✔ How many children altogether play instruments? _____

✔ Which instrument do most children play? _____

✔ Which instrument do the fewest children play? _____

✔ Which instruments do you play or want to learn to play?

_____

Text Feature

Graphs

A **bar graph** is a kind of picture. It shows you **amounts**, or numbers, of things at a glance. Think of all the words it would take to say the same thing!

Step 1 **Read the title to learn what information the graph shows.**

The bar graph below shows how high the temperature gets in some places.

Step 2 **Read the labels on the bar graph.**

The labels on the bottom are **words**. They tell **what** places the graph is about. The labels on the side are **numbers** for temperatures.

Step 3 **Find the information that each bar gives.**

Step 4 **Compare and contrast the information on the graph.**

Hot Days, Cool Animals

Scientists now know how the desert lark keeps cool in the Arabian Desert in Africa. The desert can get as hot as 122 degrees Fahrenheit (FA-run-hite)! When the temperature rises, this bird goes into the cool burrow of the Egyptian spiny-tailed lizard. The lizard doesn't seem to mind sharing its home. There is plenty of room for all.

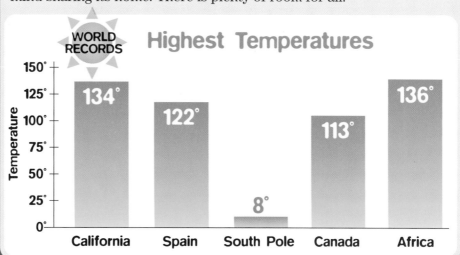

WORLD RECORDS

Highest Temperatures

Temperature

150°
125°
100°
75°
50°
25°
0°

134° — California
122° — Spain
8° — South Pole
113° — Canada
136° — Africa

Before You Read

Preview the article. Check (✔) the special features it has.

__ title
__ caption
__ flow chart
__ pronunciations
__ bar graph
__ time line

As You Read

- Did you read the title of the bar graph?
  ❏ Yes ❏ No

- What do the blue bars show?
  ❏ males
  ❏ females

- Explain how you read the graph.

After You Read

1. Are there more male or female tamarins?

2. Which zoos have less than six tamarins?

PAIR SHARE Why are zoos trying to help the tamarins?

Zoos Help Out

This baby monkey grew up healthy with the help of a zoo. It is a golden lion tamarin (TAM-uh-rin). This kind of monkey is **endangered**, or close to dying out forever. Zoos work hard to help endangered animals, like this tamarin, every day.

Baby golden lion tamarin at the National Zoo in Washington, D.C.

The bar graph shows how many **male** and **female** golden lion tamarins are at some U.S. zoos.

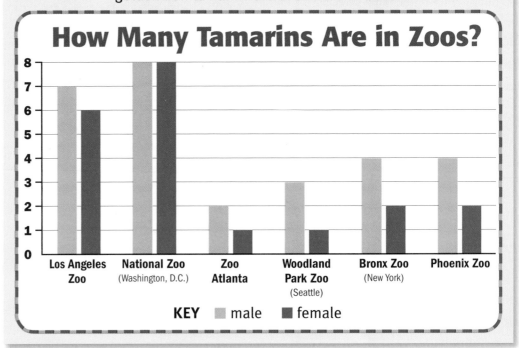

How Many Tamarins Are in Zoos?

Los Angeles Zoo — National Zoo (Washington, D.C.) — Zoo Atlanta — Woodland Park Zoo (Seattle) — Bronx Zoo (New York) — Phoenix Zoo

KEY ■ male ■ female

On Your Own

The bar graph below shows how long most big cats are. Use your graph-reading skills to learn how the cats are alike and different. Remember to:

Step 1 Read the bar graph title and labels.

Step 2 Study the graph carefully.

Step 3 Compare and contrast the information it shows. For example, ask yourself, "How much longer than the jaguar is the tiger?"

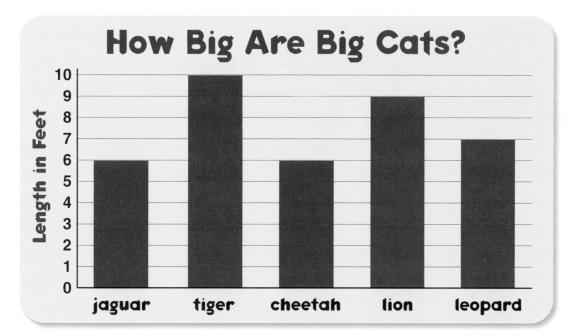

Write three questions that could be answered by the bar graph. Use the words in the list. When you're done, trade papers with a partner. Answer each other's questions.

How long
longer longest
shorter shortest
Which

1. _____

_____

2. _____

_____

3. _____

_____

Cause/Effect

Before You Read

Vocabulary Use the words to fill in each concept.

environment
recycle   **hazard**

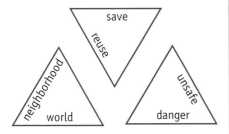

save
reuse
neighborhood
world
unsafe
danger

As You Read

Text Structure The writer of this article tells what things happen **(effects)** and why they happen **(causes)**.

Text Feature How does the bar graph help you understand the article?

After You Read

1. What can happen when people litter?

2. What can you do on Earth Day and every day to help our environment?

3. Which activity uses the most water?

KIDS HELP THE EARTH

Earth Day is a day to care about the Earth. Kids across America are making every day Earth Day.

KIDS TEACHING KIDS

Chance Ruder, age 8, holds up a plastic bag in front of 150 kids at Sea World, in San Antonio, Texas. "Can you name this **hazard**, or danger?" asks Chance. He tells them that when people litter, these bags end up in the ocean—and in the stomachs of sea turtles who think the bags are jellyfish. This causes danger to ocean animals. Chance thinks kids can have an effect on the **environment** and animals.

So, Chance learns about the hazards ocean animals face. Chance teaches what he learns to kids, "When we grow up, we must think differently if these animals are to survive."

Here, Chance learns about the special needs of penguins. He will then teach kids what people can do to help penguins survive.

Recycling Business

Kevin Harris doesn't like to see trash piling up in his neighborhood. "It upsets me," he says. So, Kevin started his own business to **recycle** things. Things that are recycled can be used again or made into other things.

Every week, Kevin picks up glass, plastic, soda cans, and paper from family and friends. Then he washes, sorts, and takes them to a recycling center. Now the neighborhood is cleaner. Kevin has even saved money for college. "I've made about $300 so far," he says.

Kevin Harris started his business in St. Louis, Missouri, when he was 9 years old.

Cleaning Up

What do tires, kitchen sinks, and soda cans have in common? They are all things Lindsay Gilbert, age 7, has helped fish out of the Pine River in Goodells, Michigan. This trash has caused the river to become polluted.

So, each fall and spring, Lindsay and her local 4-H Club clean the river. "It makes me feel happy because I am making the water a healthy place for the fish to live," says Lindsay.

Lindsay (bottom left) stands with her 4-H Club. There are around 93,000 4-H Clubs across the U.S.

WE USE WATER!

Liters of Water Each person uses each day

Activity	Liters
drinking	~2
showering	60
bathing	100
brushing teeth	10
washing hands	30
washing dishes	43

Cause/Effect

Reread "Kids Help the Earth." Fill in the chart to show what has happened to our environment (cause) and how kids have helped (effect).

Cause	Effect

 Use the organizer above to retell "Kids Help the Earth" in your own words. Remember to include the cause of each problem and the effects.

Writing Frame

Use the information in your graphic organizer to fill in the writing frame.

We can help our environment in many ways.

One thing we can do is _____.

We need to do this because _____

_____.

Another thing we can do is _____

_____.

We need to do this because _____

_____.

We can also _____.

We need to do this because _____

_____.

All these things help our environment.

 Use the writing frame above as a model to write a paragraph how you help, or could help, the environment. Be sure to include causes and effects in your paragraph.

Text Feature

Time Lines

What happened? and *When?* are two questions you might ask when you are learning about a new topic or a famous person. To answer those questions, you could look at a time line. A **time line** is a kind of diagram. It shows real events and the dates on which they happened. The facts on a time line appear in order.

Step 1 Read the title to find out what the time line shows.

The title tells the topic or time in history covered on the time line. The time line below shows events in the life of Martin Luther King, Jr.

Step 2 Find the starting and ending dates.

Read the time line from left to right. The earliest date is always the first one on the time line.

Step 3 Read the caption for each date.

The captions tell about each event. The captions on this time line tell the most important dates in the life of Martin Luther King, Jr.

Practice Your Skills!

1. (Circle) the date King was born.

2. Put an **X** on the date King died.

3. When was his "I Have a Dream" speech?

PAIR SHARE What happened to King in the 1960s?

Martin Luther King, Jr.

1929 Born in Atlanta, Georgia, on January 15.

1947 Becomes a minister.

1963 Tells crowd of 250,000 at Lincoln Memorial, "I Have a Dream."

1968 Is shot and killed on April 4 in Memphis, Tennessee.

1920   1930   1940   1950   1960

1934 By age 5, knows Bible passages and hymns by heart.

1955 Leads the Montgomery, Alabama, bus boycott.

1964 Gets the Nobel Peace Prize for civil rights.

MY STORY BY RUBY BRIDGES

Back when I was in kindergarten, I went to school with other African-American students. African-American and white children were not allowed to go to school together. Can you believe it?

Our parents went to court to ask that all children go to the same schools. The judge said that we could!

Now I had to go to a new school. I was the only African-American child to go to this school. Many white people were angry when I went there. The president of our country sent guards to walk with me and keep me safe.

Many white parents took their children out of school. They didn't want their children to be in the same class that I was in. I was the only child in my class. My teacher, Mrs. Henry, became my best friend.

By the end of the year, some parents sent their children back to school. I made friends!

The next year, many more African-American children went to the school. Children of every color have gone to the school ever since.

I am proud that I helped to make our schools open to all children.

RUBY'S TIME LINE

Spring 1960
Ruby and other black kindergarten children are tested to see which should be sent to the white schools.

Summer, 1960
Ruby is one of only a few black children who passed the test. Ruby has been chosen to go to William Frantz Public School, a white school.

September, 1960
Lawyers fight in court to stop Ruby and the other black children from going to the white schools.

November 14, 1960
Ruby attends her first day of school at the white school. Protesters fill the streets. She is the only student in school that day. Ruby sits in the office with her mother all day.

November 15, 1960
Ruby meets Mrs. Henry, her first-grade teacher. Ruby is still the only student in school.

December 5, 1960
Now only 18 children are attending Ruby's school. None of them are in Ruby's class. The parents of the other children still won't allow them to go to school with Ruby.

Spring, 1961
It is near the end of the school year. Ruby gets to meet a few white children in other classes. She is still the only student in her class.

On Your Own

Make a time line. You can use The Facts to help you. Here's how:

Step 1 Read the time line title.

Step 2 Find the starting and ending dates.

Step 3 Use The Facts to write a label for each date.

The Star-Spangled Banner

| 1779 | 1796 | 1814 | 1843 | 1931 |

Here's more information for the time line: In 1802, Key became a lawyer in Washington, D.C. Where would you add this date? Write a label for the new date.

Text Feature

Time Lines

A **time line** is a special kind of diagram. It shows real events and the dates on which they happened. The facts on a time line appear in order, from the earliest date to the latest.

Step 1 **Read the title to find out what the time line shows.**

The time line below shows the years in which some things were invented.

Step 2 **Find the starting and ending dates.**

Read the time line from left to right. The earliest date is always the first one. On this time line, it's 1900. What's the last date?

Step 3 **Read the caption for each date.**

The captions tell about each event. The captions on this time line give the dates for important inventions.

Practice Your Skills!

1. Circle the first invention.

2. Draw a box around the last invention shown.

3. When was TV invented?

PAIR SHARE What was invented in the 1920s? Which of these inventions do you use?

Great Inventions

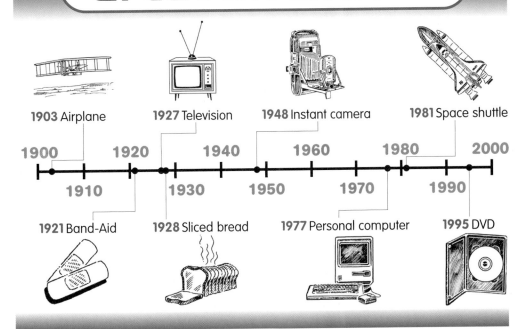

1903 Airplane   1927 Television   1948 Instant camera   1981 Space shuttle

1900   1920   1940   1960   1980   2000

1910   1930   1950   1970   1990

1921 Band-Aid   1928 Sliced bread   1977 Personal computer   1995 DVD

Practice Your Skills!

Before You Read

Preview the article. Check (✔) the special features it has.

___ captions
___ boldfaced words
___ flow chart
___ pictures
___ time line

As You Read

- Did you follow the dates in order?
  ❏ Yes   ❏ No

- How many events are on the time line?
  ❏ 5   ❏ 11

- Explain how you read the time line.

After You Read

1. What was invented first—the telephone or the elevator?

2. How did light bulbs make things safer?

PAIR SHARE How did the light bulb change the way people lived?

GREAT SCIENTISTS

Thomas Edison

Long ago, people used candles and oil lamps for lights. In the late 1800s, several people invented electric lights. One of them was Thomas Edison. He invented a **light bulb** in 1878 that worked better and lasted longer than other electric lights. It improved safety and helped people see better at night.

Edison worked on the light bulb up to 20 hours a day for one year.

Bell's great invention was based on his work helping deaf, or hearing-impaired, people.

Alexander Graham Bell

Alexander Graham Bell invented the **telephone** in 1876. For the first time, people could talk to each other even when they were far apart. Soon people in Boston could speak with people in New York. By the 1930s, telephones linked people all around the world.

GREAT INVENTIONS

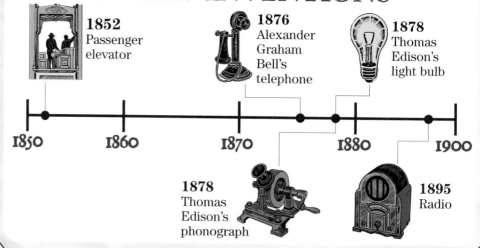

1852 Passenger elevator

1876 Alexander Graham Bell's telephone

1878 Thomas Edison's light bulb

1878 Thomas Edison's phonograph

1895 Radio

1850   1860   1870   1880   1900

On Your Own

Make a time line. Show the important events in your life. Here's how:

Step 1 Give the time line a title.

Step 2 Write five important dates or events in order.

Step 3 Add a label for each important date. Add pictures, too.

Title: _____

Sequence

Practice Your Skills!

Before You Read

Vocabulary Use the words to help fill in the word web.

attention   blind   guide dog

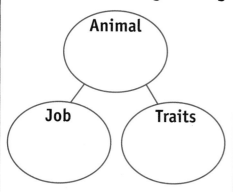

As You Read

Text Structure The author of this article describes the steps a dog follows to become a guide dog. As you read, <u>underline</u> words such as **first** and **then**. These words give clues about the order in which events happen.

Text Feature How does the time line help you understand the article?

After You Read

1. Why is Remi taught to wait for food?

2. What are important traits for guide dogs?

3. What will Remi do after she leaves Lindsay?

Guide Dog Lessons

Guide dogs help blind people. The dogs lead the people where they need to go. How do dogs learn this job? People like Lindsay teach them!

Guide dogs must learn not to run ahead of their blind owners. Here, Lindsay teaches Remi not to run ahead.

Most dogs go bonkers for food! Guide dogs can't, though. They must stay calm and pay attention to their blind owner.

That's why Lindsay teaches Remi to wait for food. Remi will only eat when Lindsay says, "OK."

Guide dogs lead their owners through crowds. Remi must get used to crowds. That's why Lindsay brings Remi to her classroom. Look how quietly Remi sits near all those people!

What's Next for Remi?

First, she will leave Lindsay and go to guide-dog school.

Then, she will train at the school for about seven months. She still has a lot to learn.

Finally, if she is good at her job, she will become a guide dog. (If not, she will become a pet!) Good luck, Remi!

This is what guide dogs do.

Guide Dog Training

The dog goes to live with a family for training.

The dog leaves the family. It goes back to guide-dog school for more training.

(1 year)   (2 years)

months 0 1 2 3 4 5 6 7 8 9 10 11 12 13 14 15 16 17 18 19 20 21 22 23 24

The dog is born.

The dog visits guide-dog school. It gets a "report card" with tasks it needs to work on. It keeps training with the family.

The dog goes home with a blind person.

Sequence

Reread "Guide Dog Lessons." Fill in the graphic organizer to show the events in the life of a guide dog.

A Guide Dog in Training

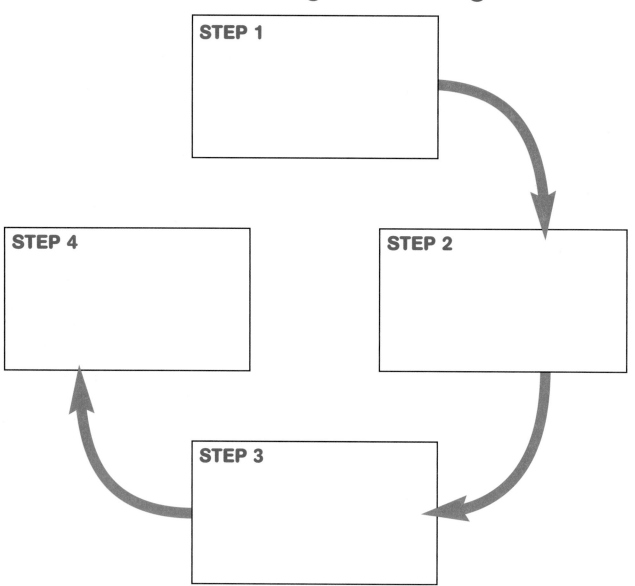

STEP 1

STEP 2

STEP 3

STEP 4

Retell Use the flow chart above to retell "Guide Dog Lessons" in your own words. Remember to tell the events in the order in which they happen. Think about what happens first, second, next, and last. Include these "signal" words in your retelling.

Writing Frame

Use the information in your flow chart to fill in the writing frame.

A dog goes through many steps before it can become a guide dog.

First, _____

_____

_____ .

Next, _____

_____

_____ .

Then, _____

_____

_____ .

Finally, _____

_____

_____ .

 Use the writing frame above as a model to tell the sequence of steps in how to get from one place to another, such as from your school to your home.

LET'S NAVIGATE

Follow the five easy steps when you read nonfiction text.

5 EASY STEPS

Step ① Preview
Read the title, introduction, and headings. Think about what they tell you.

Step ② Prepare
Say to yourself, "This article is going to be about _____. What do I already know?"

Step ③ Read
Carefully read the article.

Step ④ Use the Tools
Stop at special features, such as the special type and the graphics. Ask yourself,

- Why is this here?
- What does it tell me?
- How does it connect to the article?

Step ⑤ Retell/Connect
Retell what you learned. Think about how it connects to your life and the world.

THE AMAZING OCTOPUS

The octopus is an awesome ocean animal. It can be as HUGE as 30 feet or as tiny as 1 inch in length. What makes this creature so amazing?

Body Parts

An octopus has 8 arms that it uses to swim and to catch food. An octopus has suction cups on the back of its arms.

Suction cups help the octopus grab a meal, such as crabs, clams, and fish. If an octopus loses an arm, it can grow another one. This is called **regeneration** (ree-gen-uh-RAY-shun). A starfish can do the same thing.

An octopus has no bones, so its body is soft and squishy. This allows it to squeeze into small spaces. An octopus can squeeze into a seashell! This helps the octopus chase food even into little cracks.

Survival Skills

Octopuses have many ways to avoid their enemies. An octopus can change colors as **camouflage** (KAM-uh-flahzh), a way to blend in with its surroundings. That way, its enemies can't see it. And, in the blink of an eye, it can make its skin bumpy. To an enemy, the octopus looks like just another rock!

An octopus can also squirt purple-black ink at its enemies. The enemy can't see the octopus through the ink, and the octopus can quickly swim away to safety.

TEXT STRUCTURES

Cause/ Effect

cause → effect

Problem/ Solution

problem → solution

Sequence

step 1　step 2　step 3　step 4

Description

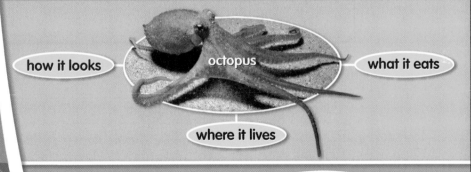

how it looks — octopus — what it eats

where it lives

Compare/ Contrast

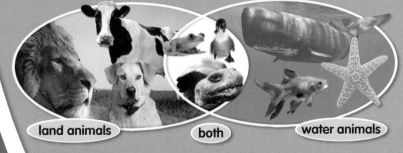

land animals　both　water animals

Sequence

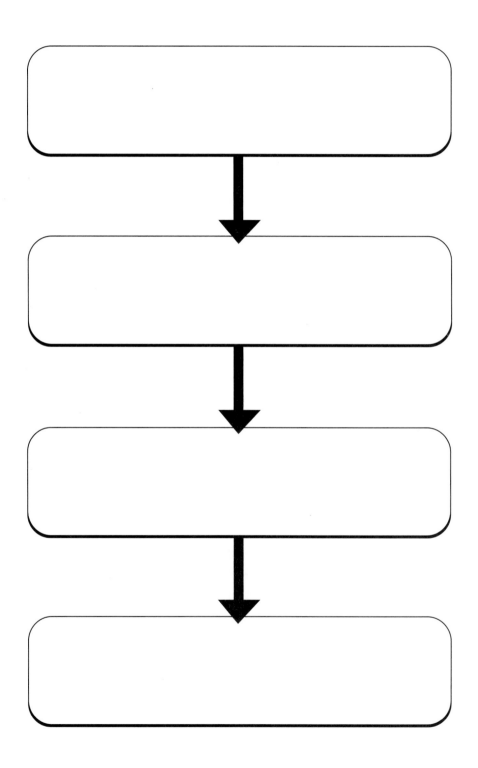

Compare/Contrast

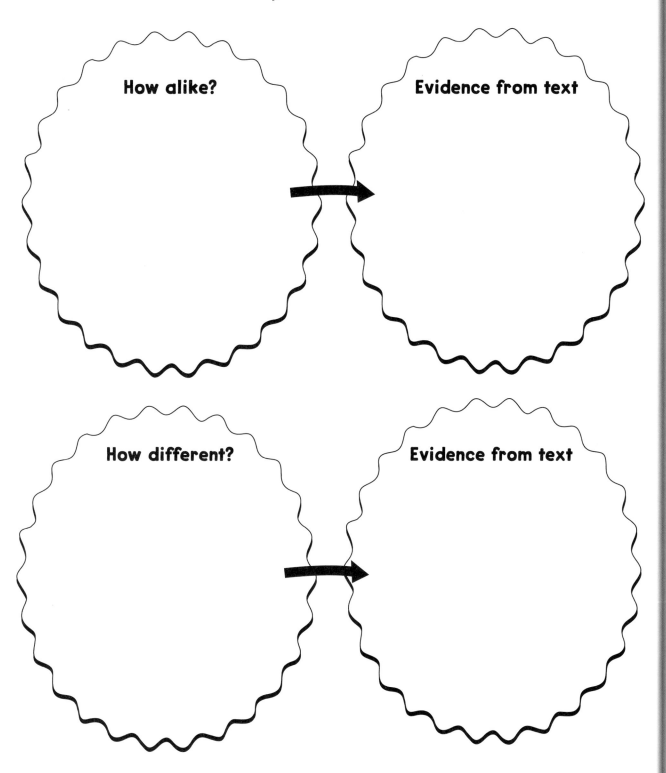

How alike?

Evidence from text

How different?

Evidence from text

Cause/Effect

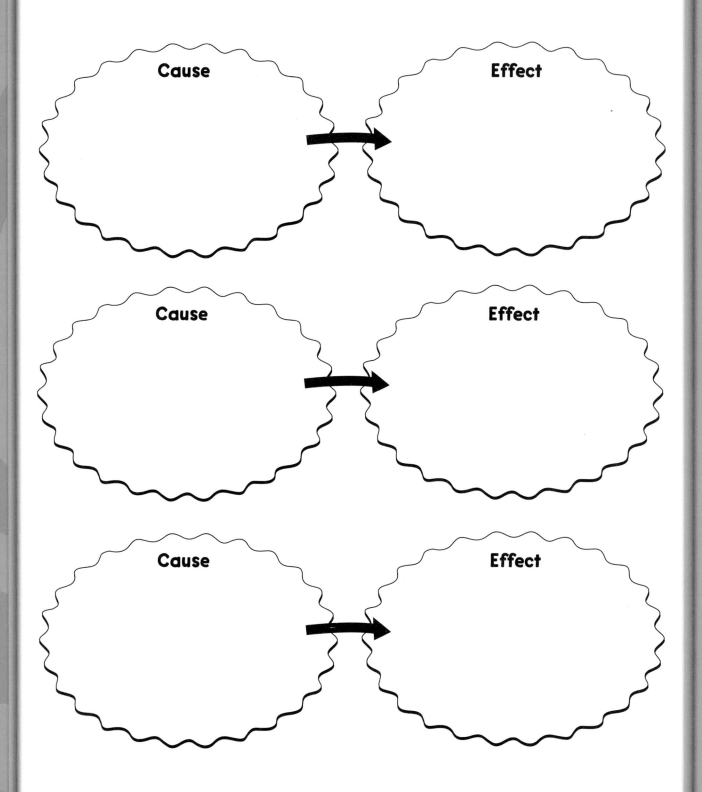

Cause

Effect

Cause

Effect

Cause

Effect

Problem/Solution

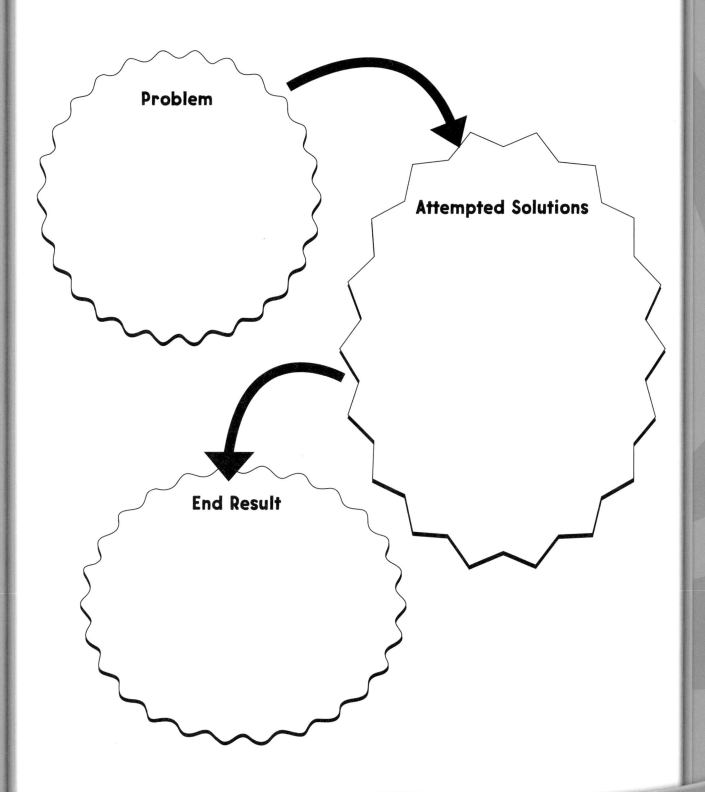

Problem

Attempted Solutions

End Result

Description

Main Idea _____
_____

Detail 1 _____
_____

Detail 2 _____
_____

Detail 3 _____
_____

Detail 4 _____
_____

Credits

Text: "Look What Animal Teeth Can Do," "Alaskan Animals Change With the Seasons," "A Wampanoag Homesite," "Oh Wow! A Powwow," "Endangered Animals Get Help," "Animals Need Trees," "What's in a Rain Forest Tree?," "Stamp of Excellence," "Meat-Eating Plants," "Pilgrim Children," "Groundhog Burrow," "Columbus's Trip," "From Grapevine to Jelly Jar," "Making Crayons," "A Ladybug's Life Cycle," "Take a Trip, Butterflies," "Just Add Water," "Seeds on the Go," "Flag Day," "Chinese New Year," "Amazing Rain," "Women Inventors," "Women Scientists of Today," "Those Amazing Spiders," "Today's Cool Fire Tools," "Helicopters Help Out," "My Dad Is a Park Ranger," "Be a Dino Detective," "Chocolate Comes From Trees," "Water in Winter," "The Power of Weather," "Before They Were President," "Meet Gary Soto," "Hot Days, Cool Animals," "Zoos Help Out," "Kids Help the Earth," "My Story, By Ruby Bridges," and "Guide Dog Lessons" are reprinted from SCHOLASTIC NEWS. Copyright © 2000, 2001, 2002, 2003, 2004 by Scholastic Inc. Reprinted by permission. "Space Suits" and "How a Butterfly Grows" are reprinted from TEACHING STUDENTS TO READ NONFICTION: GRADES 2–4. Published by Scholastic Inc. Copyright © 2004 by Alice Boynton and Wiley Blevins. Reprinted by permission. "It's a Frog's Life," "How Animals' Body Parts Help Them Survive," "Weather in Our Country," "Great Scientists," and "Great Inventions" are reprinted from CONTENT AREA READING: SCIENCE. Copyright © Scholastic Inc. Reprinted by permission. "Time Lines" is adapted from AMERICAN HISTORY TIME LINES published by Scholastic Inc. Copyright © 1996 by Susan Washburn Buckley. Reprinted by permission. "Great Inventions" is reprinted from LIFT-THE-FLAP TIMELINES: AMERICAN HISTORY. Published by Scholastic Inc. Copyright © 2004 by Alyse Sweeney. Reprinted by permission.

Images: Cover: Tree frog © Tim Davis/Corbis; Firefighter © Rubberball/Jupiter Images; Crayons © Royalty-Free/Corbis; Butterfly © Darrell Gulin/Corbis. Page 4: Wayne Lunch/DRK Photo. Page 5: (map) Mapman/Scholastic; (photos, clockwise from top left) Norbert Rosing/National Geographic Image Collection; Jim Brandenburg/Minden; Stouffer Prod./Animals Animals; Eastcott-Momatiuk/Animals Animals. Page 7: Ted Curtin/Plimoth Plantation; (inset) Judith Canty/Stock Boston. Page 8: (top) Mary Pierpoint; (bottom, from left) Lindsay Hebberd; Cleve Bryant/PhotoEdit; Michael Newman/PhotoEdit. Page 9: Maurizio Gambarini/dpa/Corbis. Page 10: Lynn M. Stone/ DRK. Page 11: (clockwise from top) Robert & Linda Mitchell Photography; Tom Brakefield/DRK; Erwin & Peggy Bauer/Bruce Coleman. Page 14: Ellen Appleby. Page 15: (map) Jim McMahon; (illustration) Karen Beckhardt; (photos, clockwise from top right) Tui de Roy/Minden Pictures; Stephen J. Krasemann/Photo Researchers; Tom Brakefield/Bruce Coleman Inc.; Jim Markowich & Sandy Mayer; Eyewire/Getty Images. Page 16: Lisa Falkenstern. Page 17: Courtesy USPS; Page 18: (top left & center) Brian LaRossa; (bottom, from left) Flickr.com/Wallace Gobetz; Photolink/Getty. Page 21: (bottom) E.R. Degginger/Dembins. Page 24: Photodisc. Page 25: Ted Curtin Photography. Pages 26–27: Nathan Hale. Page 28: Tom Leonard. Page 29: Jason Robinson. Pages 30–31: Tom Leonard; (globe) Mapman/Scholastic. Page 34: (steps 1 & 2) Welch's; (steps 3 & 5) Grafton Smith; (step 4) Michael Myers/Welch's. Page 35: Gale Zucker/www.gzucker.com. Page 37: Patricia J. Wynne. Page 38: (photos, clockwise from top left) Rogers/Photo Researchers; Dwight R. Kuhn/Bruce Coleman; Steve Hopkin/Getty Images; Nuridsany et Perennou/Photo Researchers. Page 39: Lisa Falkenstern. Page 40: Dan Guravich/Photo Researchers. Page 41: (left) John Henry Williams/Bruce Coleman; (right) Danny Lehman/Corbis. Page 44: George H. H. Huey. Page 45: (top photo) David Cavagnaro; (bottom photos) Peter Arnold; (illustration) John Carrozza. Page 46: Scott Camazine/Photo Researchers. Page 47: (photo) John Michael/International Stock Photo. Page 48: (from top) Brian LaRossa; A. Ramey/PhotoEdit; AP Wide World. Page 49: Don Smetzer/Getty Images. Page 50: (from top) Bryan Peterson/Getty Images; Ron Dahlquist/Superstock; (illustration) Rita Lascaro. Page 51: (reservoir) Teake Zuidema/The Image Works; (girl) Bryan Peterson/Foodpix; (chameleon) Dwight Kuhn/Bruce Coleman Inc.; (clouds, from top) David R. Frazier/Photo Researchers; Tom Bean/Corbis; DPA/Dembinsky Photo Associates; Charles O'Rear/Corbis. Page 54: Anne-Moore Weego. Page 55: (photo top) Matthew Cavanaugh; (photo bottom) Wilford Harewood Photography; (illustrations) Brian LaRossa. Page 57: (from top) Pam Langer; Animals Animals/Brian Miller. Page 58: (from top, clockwise) Dan Sudial/Photo Researchers; Photodisc via SODA; Kenneth W. Fink/Photo Researchers. Page 60: (left) Richard T. Nowitz/Corbis. Page 61: (right) Bruce Ayres/Getty Images. Page 64: Brian LaRossa. Page 65: (illustration) Brian LaRossa; (map) Mapman/Scholastic. Page 66: Brian LaRossa. Page 67: (photo) Yves Forestier/Corbis Sygma; Mapman/Scholastic. Page 68: Tom Spitz/Getty; Mapman/Scholastic. Pages 70–71: (dinosaur) Brian Cooley; (Hendrickson) G. Papadakis; (map) Mapman/Scholastic. Pages 74: (photo) Greg Pease/Tony Stone; (illustrations) Ellen Appleby. Page 75: (photo bottom) Robert Frerck/Tony Stone; (illustrations) Ellen Appleby. Page 78: (clockwise from top left) Tom Mareschal/Getty Images; Jim Zuckerman/Corbis; Royalty-Free/Corbis; Mike Schroder/Peter Arnold, Inc. Pages 80–81: Craig Orback. Page 85: George Olson. Page 90: Bob French/SeaWorld/San Antonio. Page 91: (left) John Rehg/Liaison. Page 94: (from left) Francis Miller/Time Life Pictures; AP Photo; (bottom) Ted Spiegel/Corbis. Page 95: Michael Garland. Page 96: Corbis. Page 97: Teresa Southwell. Page 98: (photos) Bettmann/Corbis; (illustrations) Teresa Southwell. Pages 100–101: Gilles Mingasson/Getty Images. Page 104: (from top) David Fleetham/Pacific Stock; © Mark Conlin/SeaPics.com; Eiichi Korasawa/Photo

Editor: Mela Ottaiano
Cover Design: Jorge J. Namerow